Alexa

For Richard Campbell

— we were all young
once — honest!

Best wishes

Brian Linton

Alexa

The life and death of an Austin 7 Ruby
By Brian Milton

An account of a drive across Africa in 1968/9 in a 1937 Austin 7 Ruby to marry a girl in Johannesburg.

The Austin 7, called Alexa, did not survive the journey.

ATLANTIC

ALGERIA

SAHARA DESERT

MALI

NIGER

NIGERIA

Algiers

Guardaia

El Golea

In salah

Ptomaine poisoning, crashed here

Tamannrasset

In Guezzam

Boys left me

Ran out of water

Ran out of water here, too

Agadez

Half-shaft incident

Zinder

Kano

Ceuta

Chechaoueh

Met Cowboys

BY 1937 AUSTIN RUBY SEVEN
RUBY SALOON ("ALEXA")
ACROSS AFRICA
NOVEMBER 13, 1968 - FEBRUARY 7, 1969

MEDITERRANEAN

LIBYA

EGYPT

SUDAN

Ft Lamy, Chad (Ndjamena)
Lost piston here

...dugeri

Banzyville
Broke timing case
Malaria struck
(Bebronne's base)

Bossangoa

Bangui

Yakoma

Buta   Paulis (Isiro)

Aketi

...EROON

Molegbwe
Consecration of
congolese bishop
Lost brakes

Bumba

Mungbere
(Alexa died here)

Kampala, Uganda
Entebbe, Uganda

Published in the United Kingdom in 2009 by
Burning Daylight Publications,
2 Cyprus Street,
London E2 0NN, England

First Edition, November, 2009 – 500 copies

British Library Cataloguing in Publication Data

ISBN 978-0-9555452-1-4
Copyright © 2009 Brian Milton

Cover and page design: orbitgraphic.co.uk

Printed and bound in England by ImprintDigital.net

www.brian-milton.com

 **Alexa**

Previous publications:

Dalgety Flyer, published by Bloomsbury, 1990, about an eventful microlight flight from London to Australia. Republished in a condensed version by Reader's Digest in 1991. A 25-minute TV programme on the flight was produced by ITN, called 'On a Wing and a Prayer and a Sponsor' and seen in 23 countries. Video on www.brian-milton.com.

Global Flyer, published by Mainstream, 1999, about the first microlight flight around the world. Re-published in paperback by New European Publications (Travel) in 2003. Featured in BBC TV programme *'Hardtalk'*, and four half-hour television programmes on the Discovery Channel called 'A Microlight Odyssey'. Video on www.brian-milton.com.

Chasing Ghosts, published by New European Publications (Travel) in 2001, about a failed attempt in a microlight to fly non-stop across the Atlantic. Featured in an hour long television programme on the Discovery Channel called 'Escape by Microlight'. Video on www.brian-milton.com

Another Sisyphus, a novel, published by Burning Daylight Publications in 2007, about a British-born Muslim suicide bomber who kills 22 Londoners with a Tube-bomb and then has to cope, individually, with 72 virgins, not the Paradise he had expected.

Lancaster – The Biography, with Sqdn Ldr Tony Iveson DFC (617 *Dambuster* Sqdn pilot, on all 3 raids which sank the German battleship *Tirpitz*), published in May, 2009 by Andre Deutsche. In most bookshops.

Please check out Brian Milton's other books on
www.brian-milton.com

Preface

I drove Alexa across Africa and wrote about that journey forty years ago, when I was a young man. I might have made more efforts to get the book published but getting expelled from a racist *Apartheid* South Africa, working in Liberal politics in the early 1970's, and then as a full-time freelance journalist trying to buy a house and earn enough to support a family, the story fell between the cracks.

Later, for years I was possessed by hang gliding, and then flying microlights. It turned out that my view that the drive across Africa would be my 'last adventure' was wrong.

But at 2.40pm on Friday, May 30, 2008 I had what could have easily been a fatal accident but somehow wasn't. On a test flight in the flexwing microlight in which I flew around the world, seconds after take-off she started acting like a pig. Instead of landing immediately I flew a circuit at 400 feet, and then approached and put down safely. I was on the verge of asking for a second opinion when I discovered that the tip of the port sail had broken loose and the wing surface was rumpled. An eight inch split in it would have gone three inches further – and flapped with fatal results – had it not been for a line of double stitching.

After that, I thought that it was worth squaring away my affairs.

Telling Alexa's story is part of the process.

I believe the drive across Africa in Alexa helped me earn the funding from Terry Pryce at Dalgety to make the microlight flight to Australia in 1987, and the Australia flight helped convince Prince Philipp of Liechtenstein, who owned GT Global, to support me on the world flight in 1998.

It is all connected and I have written about both those adventures, but the Alexa story has never seen the light of day.

Reading it again, I am conscious that I had so little money and very few skills beyond being able to drive a car and make primitive repairs.

But I am glad I stayed true to the adventure all the way through to the end of it. It was the first adventure book I wrote, and I half-learned a lesson in keeping a decent diary when out on the road. Revisiting such diaries is now one of the pleasures in life.

As I was crossing Africa the great drive to decolonise was almost complete. I did not make it to Rhodesia where the white colonial community held out until 1980, but I did get to South Africa for a while before suffering the fate of dozens of journalists; six journalists and six priests, on average, were expelled each year. The Africans I met were trying to grasp the levers of power – there was a civil war in Nigeria at the time – without much success. I cannot say they have got any better at ruling themselves in the intervening 40 years. The roads over which I drove, however bad, were still working then; many of the places I went through, especially in the Congo, have since reverted to being Joseph Conrad's *Heart of Darkness*.

I don't think I could make a similar drive today over the same route I drove Alexa at the end of the 1960's.

I am not sure when it will ever be possible again in the future, so Alexa's fate, however insignificant, is now a piece of Africa's history.

Brian Milton, London 2009

A Crash in the Sahara

December 6th, 1968

That morning I was out of my sleeping bag at dawn, as usual. The big lidless kettle was steaming over my Primus stove, set up and watched from the tent as I smoked my first cigarette, with the daylight creeping down the small jagged hills surrounding the Sahara camp-site. I made breakfast, two cups of Algerian coffee given as a present from the director of education at In Salah a hundred and two miles north, along with porridge mixed with hot water, sugar and powdered milk and eaten raw. I finished with a lump of cheese and half a loaf of bread. The sun swung up behind me and chased away the deep night shadows. I hummed a few bars of a music-hall song between eating, with better manners than the night before, and fixed in my mind what had to be done to pack up and drive on.

My 1937 Austin 7 Ruby, called Alexa, was clear of the sand into which I had driven her for the sixth time the day before. There were gouge marks behind her rear wheels, and both pieces of chicken-netting, which I used as sand-mats, lay crumpled and familiar ten yards away. The Hoggar Trail, by which I had camped, was also marked with the tracks of a large truck which I had heard pass in the night, going south. If it had a breakdown, I might possibly catch it, I thought, but I was not eager. I liked being alone.

Before pouring hot water from the kettle into a bucket to wash and shave with, I checked over Alexa. She ate one pint of oil a day at that time, and hardly any water leaked from the radiator. I started the engine and screwed down the accelerator to warm it up at medium revs, then broke camp. For reasons of self-discipline I took a long time shaving, as if I was going to a dinner party rather than across the Sahara. At about 7.30am, I was ready to leave.

Everything was packed into the car; tent, sleeping bag, my huge old typewriter called Brunehilde, petrol and water tanks, and my little ritual performed each driving day of hanging a pair of goggles around my neck. I lit a cigarette, stepped in behind the wheel, and drove gingerly back on to the track and south towards Tamanrasset.

The morning went well. I had learned to be cautious of sand, after falling into it a dozen times. The few sand banks that blocked the track were easily negotiable, using some of the new tricks I had learned. Each time I saw sand, I drove the car as fast as possible at it, and when the wheels dragged, crashed down through the gears and slipped the clutch; we were usually able to stagger through. Alexa was one of the more sophisticated Ruby saloons, built nearly four years after the four-speed crash gear-box was modified in 1933, and with synchro-mesh from second to top gear. Thirty-two years had not adversely affected the gear-box's performance. By lunchtime I had driven 80 miles, and was feeling happy. I did not notice how hot it had become until, rounding one bend, there was a long soft bed of sand covering the track, and Alexa slewed into it and stopped.

For an hour, dressed only in jean shorts and a pair of sandals, I scrabbled about under the wheels, pulling at sand with my forearms, placing the crumpled chicken netting in front of the rear wheels, and digging. Each time I felt the car would lift clear, I started the engine, dropped into first gear, revved and swayed to and fro and cursed, and the car lolloped forward anything from two feet to – once – 14 yards.

Occasionally, I thought about the 260 miles left to Tamannrasset, but when I did I could feel myself becoming desperate, so I concentrated on measuring minutely the progress after each attempt. The yellow sun hung over the desolate surrounding countryside, the baked rock and brown clay of the Tadjemout Plateau, for the first time since I had entered the desert throwing out that blistering heat which had so haunted me in my dreams before I left London.

Twice I paced out the length of sand I still had to cover. Once I walked up to a hill to look for any future sand banks, to prepare myself for when I got past this one. At about 1.15, black flies clustered around my face and hands, I ate a Robert Jordan sandwich, thick cheese with raw onion slices in bread. Then I heard a noise and five French students came down the track in a pair of Citroen 2CVs and pushed me out of the sand within five minutes.

The afternoon was the first rough one, the first when Africa in all its natural indifference asserted itself, and I could no longer pretend, as I had to strangers, that I was an eccentric on holiday in an old car. I found myself consciously refraining from shrieking, just to take the tension away. The Frenchmen stopped for lunch at Arak, an old fortress town, after both they and I had nearly been stoned by an Arab who became violent when we did not stop and give him cigarettes. I waved and drove on. The land stretched for hundreds of miles, empty, waiting silently for me to drive over it so that, when I had done so, I would still have hundreds more miles to cover. Even thinking of Fiona Campbell, the girl I was driving down the continent to marry, became absurd, yet she usually helped to keep me going.

Three policemen, one of them a fat jolly fellow, drove up in the late afternoon while I was pouring more petrol into the fuel tank. They followed me for miles and pushed me out of the second drift of the day. As the sun was going down, I found I was no longer choosy about where I camped. Instead of passing one flat piece of land after another until the sun set, I chose the first and was immensely relieved to get out of the car.

I had the large kettle full of water going by the time the French students arrived. They decided they would camp with me. I set up my tent and sleeping bag, and made coffee, while they parked their cars and dug trenches around their beds which they told me were protection against snakes and scorpions. My meal was the rest of the sardines from a huge tin I was given at In Salah, plus bread and cheese. We talked about the Common Market around my Primus, and the riots in Paris that May; I had been there as a tour director, and had been beaten by the police on the Rue St Jacques before escaping. After an hour I began to feel strange, light-stomached rather than light-headed. I thought it was probably the altitude, near to 3,000 feet. We looked over each other's cars. They were fascinated by mine – Austin 7's were rare in France – and thought the old flowered curtains I had nailed inside as roof lining were very pretty. They called Alexa *le voiture hippique*, the hippy car. We went to sleep early. They had to be in Tamanrasset the next evening to catch an aircraft to Djanet the following day and finish their holiday. I asked them to wake me in the morning and, if Alexa could keep up, I would drive on with them.

I woke up at two in the morning with a terrible pain stretched across my stomach. I had a medical box, but nothing for stomach disorders. For three hours, until I heard the Frenchman singing "God Save the Queen" at 5 o'clock, I turned and rolled, half-awake, half-asleep, just aware that I should do something, never quite able to grasp what. A Frenchman came over. I told him apologetically what was wrong. He gave me a heap of stomach powders, and within 15 seconds I had catapulted out of the tent to vomit the rotten sardines all over the desert. *Ptomaine poisoning*. It was wretched. I suffered racking pains across my stomach which felt taut as a drum, a first-class case of diarrhoea and the overwhelming urge to reach Tamanrasset, 200 miles away, before nightfall.

I managed to break camp, and told the Frenchmen to go on without me. In a funny way I was afraid to take help, and wanted to deal with the poisoning in the same way as a cat does when it is hurt. With frequent halts to curl over my stomach, I managed to pack up camp, and was on the road by 7am. If I had not been so groggy, I would have noticed that my iron rule about always shaving was absurd in the circumstances. As host the night before, I had been too liberal with my supply of water, and there was little left. After an hour's driving and a few cigarettes I realised I might have to spend another night camping alone. With what water I had, my ration for the day was two mouthfuls every two hours, at 9.15, 11.15 and so on. As it happened, I need not have considered further than 11.15.

Driving in the desert was not boring. There was too much to do, each lump in the track to be negotiated, each furrow heaped with curses and eased through. But because of the shocking state of the track, my eyes become accustomed to searching only 20 yards ahead of the car, for each piece of track was unique and needed careful driving. And normally, there was nothing to look at but hillock and rock and sand. The awareness of space and my own solitude usually came in the absolute stillness of the night.

However, in the 430 miles between In Salah and Tamanrasset there is a stretch of perhaps 25 miles of tarmac road, starting at a former Foreign Legion fort called In Ekker. The road wandered between hills with cheap stark huts perched in clusters on the slopes, and thick barbed wire divided it from the desert proper. I was relieved to drive once again without the awful hammering of the dirt track, and I was curious. I drove up to 35 mph and forgot the regular stomach cramps, down a long hill, around a corner and up again sharply towards a red fortress which, like Fort Mirabel, 500 miles north, was right out of Beau Geste.

There was, incongruously, a sign that said *Stop*. Twenty yards later a heavy steel barrier pole lay across the road. At 12.15 I saw the pole for a split second before we smashed into it. I remember hearing what I thought was glass breaking and some thumps and then a loud crash, and the car stopped...

CHAPTER 1
Origins of the Journey

I had found Alexa in 1965 in a back garden in Stoke-on-Trent where she had been lying for six months. I bought her for £25, used her for two years, not always legally, and grew very fond of her. Then I had no money for a while, so she rotted away for nine months in Greenwich.

I met Fiona Campbell at a bridge game early in 1967. She is as tall as I am, 5 feet 9 inches, slim, with curly brown hair and large blue eyes. She was the daughter of a colonel in the British Army in India, Ian Campbell, from an old Scottish family, the Campbells of Saddell; Ian once told her he had joined the army to travel and play polo. Fiona's incredible zest was very attractive. She quite blithely gave me the Campbell Fairy's blessing not long after we met – on which I unfortunately lost £100 at various gaming clubs in an effort to justify her confidence in the fairy – and though she didn't know about my loss, we began to see a lot of each other.

She was to go to South Africa in August 1967. She had been born there and left as a baby, and knew nothing of the country but hearsay. I was trying to be a writer and was virtually penniless. We were serious about nothing except that we should be responsible to each other and decided to be in love until she left, and then go our separate ways. We were afraid we would lose something in prolonging it, and thought to set our limits before we began. It sounds idealistic, even cold-blooded, and I suppose it was. We used to say, as Jack London said, "the gods wouldn't laugh at us".

Fiona was one of the few women I had met who thought Alexa was a beautiful car. I promised that, when I left England again, I would leave the car at the Isle of Wight with her parents, and she could have it when she returned.

She took a boat to South Africa – our resolution not to tie each other down unbroken – and I found a job parking cars to pay off some small debts and save money. Mr Alistair Miller, then Governor of Parkhurst Prison and a friend of Fiona's family, lent me his cottage on the west coast of Ireland near Bantry Bay for the winter. I wanted to finish writing some plays and novels. Alexa was parked in Greenwich, her engine stripped, and in October I arrived at Alistair's small stone cottage near the village of Schull with a typewriter, 24 books, and written exhortations to myself to work hard.

I lived alone in the cottage, halfway up a mountain with the wind and rain and occasional mists. During the ten weeks I spent there, I decided I wanted to marry Fiona and wrote asking for her hand. After a month, she accepted.

We thought we would get married in England, but Fiona became involved in so much in South Africa, and she seemed to like it there, that in March of 1968 I wrote that I would go out to her, rather than she come to me. Secretly, I had been restless, afraid that I would go through my twenties without one passable story collected to tell my grandchildren. Marriage was a terrifying prospect, and I wanted, so to speak, to take an antidote to it, and present the result to Fiona when I arrived. Being alone in Ireland had laid the germ of an idea that reached fruition on May 8, back in England. I would drive Alexa across Africa and give her to Fiona.

Through the summer of that year, I worked as a tour director, guiding Americans around Europe. From four tours

I was able to save $300 in traveller's cheques which I left in Paris, and $400 to put into getting the car ready and buying supplies. I had also, in a naïve bid for married responsibility, bought $250 worth of shares, which were difficult to touch. I had expected a fifth tour, but found myself on the wrong side of company politicians at a change of operations director, and it fell through.

At first, I thought two weeks' work would be enough to prepare Alexa. In the Spring, helped by an an old school friend called Colin Hunter, I had stripped the engine, re-metalled the big ends (the engine dated before March 1937, when shell bearings were introduced) and bought four new pistons and rings. I expected to see the engine together in two days. Then a condenser was needed for the radiator, some new springs, spare tyres, gaskets, points, plugs and so on, a new canvas roof screwed on, the electrics re-wired – that, I thought, would be it. I would take Alexa up to Scotland on a 2,000-mile test run in September, and leave at the end of that month.

My knowledge of cars at that time stretched as far as changing plugs, and helping someone grind valves in. My innocence was at least understandable.

On August 19, I made the first of numerous journeys by public transport from Kensington to Greenwich. It took two weeks to assemble the engine, guided by Colin whenever he could find the time. Every spare part I needed necessitated another journey by bus to a shop up in Kennington. In all, it was a dismal beginning.

My first expected deadline for the car's engine to start was September 3rd. Colin Hunter helped me get the engine into the car. We had trouble with the gearbox, which took two days to fit correctly. All the wires were joined up, the radiator connected by hoses, oil was bought, plugs fitted; we became excited. My starter motor didn't work then, so Colin cranked the engine while I turned on the ignition and pumped the accelerator. Nothing.

We tied my car to his and pulled her halfway around Greenwich. Not even a cough. Colin thought the timing might be wrong, but when we lifted the engine head and he checked the valve risings while I cranked, it seemed fine. It became too dark to do anything else, and I dejectedly took the trains home.

Colin, a policeman, was on late shift the next day. I sat in the car while he dressed and had breakfast. Though I twiddled things and thought about what was wrong, I did not know enough about cars to correct anything. There was a small garage in Circus Road called Harris Autos, five minutes walk from the block of police flats where Alexa was parked. I had had my radiator, starter motor and various re-conditioning jobs done there. After trying vainly for an hour to produce some life in the engine, Colin and I walked down to Harris Autos and talked to the two owner/mechanics. They said that if I brought the car down, they would have a look for me. We pushed Alexa out of the police yard and up to the garage.

Each day there was something to be done on the car, and I spent the whole day learning how to do it, or waiting for help. One mechanic, Brian Widdows, a bearded hedonist who collected women, married and unmarried, felt that I should make the trip across Africa in a Y-type Ford, which he had raced at some time in a chequered career. He was the more interested of the two, finding time each day to advise me on a new roof, or makeshift cooling devices, or better headlights. Malcolm Butcher, the other mechanic, helped when he could find the time, quietly and efficiently, a contrast to Brian with his ebullient and imaginative ideas. I was often delegated to make tea, a small price to pay for all they did.

Until Alexa was ready for the road I had no transport, and often nothing to do while waiting for help. Twice I visited Chichester's *Gypsy Moth IV* in her dock half a mile away. Colin quickly dropped out of the picture – his wife Barbara disapproved of me, worried that I would entice Colin into an adventurous life – and I saw him only a few times before I left. Brian and Malcolm had all my hopes pinned on them. I cultivated a frame of mind where I did not think too much about what would happen the day after tomorrow and just worked and waited mindlessly. If asked how I was going, I generally lied, sounding much more optimistic than I really was. In fact, the more pessimistic I became, the more people I told about the trip. That made more people to be ashamed in front of if I finally didn't go.

On September 7, Brian discovered why Alexa would not start. He took off the timing case and found the cogs on the crankshaft and camshaft were out by one tooth. I thought we would have to strip the engine again to fix this, and groaned. But he just knocked one cog off and fixed it in ten minutes. When the engine started I felt miserable for half an hour. I had expected to whoop it up and celebrate, but it was not like that. There seemed too much more to do.

To give some urgency to all my preparations, I had set a tentative date for departure, between October 10 and 20. On September 14, I wrote to Fiona….

Less than a month to go. I'm sitting in the flat after a day's reading and occasional bouts of apprehension. My routes came today from the A.A. It looks very difficult. Can I do it? Why should I? I don't know, except that I can't stop collecting spares and seeing embassies. I'm going through one of those periods when I doubt things. It was the same when I set off hitch-hiking on the road in the States, except I didn't have to make arrangements then which would make me afraid. It's rather nebulous, and now it's later in the evening, and I'm over it. The thing is, I must take this trip piecemeal, so I can handle it. It can't be handled whole. It has struck me that I'm wrong to palm off all these fears, for something I have chosen to do, upon you.

Next Friday, a belated birthday present from Brian and Malcolm, Alexa will be on the road again. We burnt off her wheel hubs yesterday, and are renewing the steering mechanism. Also, great fun too, we tore the roof off. A new four-layered roof is going on next Monday and Tuesday (there is a storm muttering angrily outside, and the Sorcerer's Apprentice is on the gramophone). Other points. The engine is fine; all the rest is being re-built. New headlamps, massive things more at home on a Bentley, are fixed on the front wings; Brian is fitting another water tank and a pump, which will cool the engine. We're putting in a multi-bladed fan. He says it will take half an hour to warm the car up with all this gear.

We're also adding more springs to the back of the car to give adequate clearance, and I'm taking a complete spare set. My brakes have been renewed. A new starter. There is some way of cooling the oil, a water-cooled sump, which I could fit too, I'm dreading the bill, but Brian seems so involved that I have a nice feeling he's going to undercharge me a lot. I couldn't have found a better man...

We put a new roof on, and though it was a jerrybuilt job and there were still leaks, it gave Alexa the appearance of a car again instead of a gutted wreck. Brian burnt off the wheel hubs to fit new kingpins, which seemed a drastic way to do things, and the way he hit them with a hammer appalled me, but everything went back together again. Each day some of the policemen in the Greenwich area stood and watched us for half an hour, sharing a cigarette and a cup of tea, and asking questions. Brian was almost like a circus ringmaster, lord of his domain, hiding his mechanical tricks beneath a cloud of confident patter. I was never sure whether Alexa did in fact have a chance, as he maintained to my face.

When the car was completed I planned a long run-in around Scotland. I wrote to Robert Nye in Edinburgh telling him of my plans, and asking if he would put me up for a couple of nights. Colin had said he would come with me, over the same route we had taken in a 1937 Rover 10 called Penelope in 1963, up to Pitlochry. That time, eight feet of exhaust pipe had fallen off the car, and fixing it with empty beer cans gummed onto the break, we became nearly incapable emptying the beer cans first. Colin manfully took the brunt of the task.

I thought perhaps the car would be ready to go by the end of September, I could wind up all my affairs, blow off to Scotland on the test run, find any faults, repair them, and then leave for Africa. But all the cooling devices we had put on to the car weren't working, and when we ran the engine in the garage, the oil pressure went straight off the clock and stayed there. The water pump was fixed by a strip of metal on to the fan pulley fitting, with tubes connecting it into the water system, but we were not sure which way the pump moved the water. Even in London, on a five mile run, the radiator boiled over. I thought I should reverse the water hoses. Brian thought the fault lay in the pump, and we wasted many days stripping the pump or just running the engine and hoping that the cooling problem would solve itself. In the end, I did reverse the hosing, and had no more trouble.

I began to have confidence in my own ability to make decisions about what might go wrong with the car. Yet... (October 7)

I'm worried. I don't want to commit suicide, so have some stipulations about driving down there. My oil pressure is far too high to leave the car as it is. I haven't even the money to go to Scotland, my brother Colin and Jay haven't yet come through with what they owe me. I do plan to bash the car as much as possible before I leave, to gain confidence in it. The main stipulation is that Austin's look at it. You know I wrote to Sir Donald Stokes, asking him if he would allow Austin's look at Alexa. I didn't ask for sponsorship, for if that was given totally it would ruin the whole purpose of the trip. Just that an experienced Austin mechanic check our work and advise me on my chances.

Other troubles, paperwork, money, morale, and the fact that Alexa failed the roadworthiness test on her brakes; these ate up the days, and my deadline came and went. I worried about the oil pressure, and drove the car up to East Anglia for a weekend and back again, without trouble, except that around 40 mph it felt fragile. I knew something was wrong, but I thought if I ran the car long enough, the oil pressure would drop. In a way, that is what happened.

On the evening of October 15, I drove over to Twickenham with a girl, Judy Entwistle, to see an American friend, Mike Winecoff, who was living on a houseboat there.

We had a few beers and talked. I knew I could not get away by 20 October, and was very upset about it. Mike had just finished writing a book with another American called Jay Jones, called *The Tool*. We talked about their book and about my forthcoming trip, and at around 1 o'clock in the morning, Judy and I left.

On the road back to Central London, Alexa seemed full of punch, and I was feeling cheerful. But driving out of Richmond, there was suddenly an awful noise. I switched the engine off, and freewheeled into a garage. Judy and I got out. I started the engine again, once more a terrible clattering, and I turned the engine off.

"That's a big-end noise," I said. "It has to be."

I called the A.A., but couldn't take their offer to tow me to their garage. I hadn't any money to pay for repairs. The A.A. man helped push the car along the road and down a side street, and then Judy and I walked home. We found a taxi in Chiswick, which took us back to Kensington. Judy paid.

CHAPTER 2
Paperwork

When I had first thought of driving through Africa, my conception of the place was that it was not much bigger than Europe. All the small maps of the world which subtly give us our perspective of this planet, and particularly those with England in the centre, show Africa sloping southwards like an inverted L, almost an afterthought to Europe. I knew the distance by air from London to Johannesburg was roughly 6000 miles, and at 1000 miles a week, I thought it might take me six weeks. This misconception lasted until July, when I bought a large map of Africa from the *Daily Telegraph*. By filling Africa with the United States, India, Europe and the British Isles, and with a million or so square miles still left over, the map brought home sharply the size of the area through which I intended to drive.

But other people had driven down before me, so why shouldn't I try? Sir Francis Chichester had recently returned from his solo journey by yacht around the world, and I had followed avidly Alec Rose's similar journey. They succeeded against greater odds than I was going to face, though their boats were probably in relatively better condition than my car. I could (and did) invoke these two men when things got bad. I believe in heroes.

In its early stages, the plan was to drive through Europe, down the east coast of the Mediterranean to Cairo, ferry up the Nile into the Sudan and then motor to East Africa. But politics destroyed that idea. Then I thought I would drive along the North African coast to Egypt, turn right and go down through the Sudan to Kenya. This was before I knew anything significant about African history. There was another route suggested by the A.A., first verbally, then confirmed when they sent me route information, which crossed both the Sahara Desert and the Congo. I was rather afraid of the Sahara, and frankly terrified of the Congo, so I hoped as long as was possible that I could drive down the East Coast.

At the Sudanese embassy to ask for a visa, I was told none were being issued for overland travellers, as there was trouble in the south of the country. The Congolese embassy was even more sinister, with a thin red-haired Englishman in a three-piece check suit who laughed and waffled that "visas are just not being issued, old boy". Looking at the map of Africa, I saw that the Sudan and Congo stretched like a bar sinister across it, cutting north from south. I would have to go through one of these two countries if I insisted on driving, and as I had the A.A. route for the Congo, I chose that country. Obviously, I would have to cross the Sahara too.

It seemed the best route was through France and Spain to Algeciras, next to Gibraltar, across the Straits of Gibraltar by ferry to Ceuta, along the north African coast through Morocco to Algiers, turn south along the trans-Sahara Hoggar Trail into Niger and then Nigeria. I hoped to reach Kano, Nigeria, by Christmas. After that, east to the Cameroons and Fort Lamy in Chad, turn south again to Bangassou in the Central African Republic (CAR), cross the Ubangui river and make a quick frightened dash over 1,400 miles through the Congo to emerge from Beni into Uganda and the safety of Kampala. From Kampala on down, I would be passing through what was once British East Africa, and I expected no trouble at all.

As an Englishman I did not need a visa for Europe,

Morocco, Algeria, Nigeria, Uganda, Kenya, Tanzania, Zambia and South Africa. Rhodesia, then three years into a white rebellion, might be a difficulty, and I thought I would make a decision whether to drive through there if I ever reached it. Visas were necessary for Niger, Chad, CAR, and the Congo. The Cameroons were easily the least neurotic of countries in Black Africa, and would issue me a police permit to cross its 60 miles of territory when I reached its border.

Thomas Cook secured visas, at a cost of 30/- (£1.50) each, for Niger, Chad and the CAR, though they turned out to be valid for 48 hours only after entry. I knew I would take longer than that to cross each country, but planned to extend the visas at each border, and thought to argue the case if I was ever stopped. The Congolese embassy was adamant, even to Cooks – no visas. How then did other people cross Africa? Admittedly the Belgians had gone, and one heard murderous tales about towns such as Buta and Kisangani, but surely it was quiet now? Again, I would try for a visa at the borders. The problem of getting to South Africa if the Congolese refused to issue me a visa, and I was stuck with Alexa in the middle of Africa, I shelved to worry about later. I had an awful lot of other things to worry me just then.

All this knowledge and the action of getting visas took a considerable time to acquire. Even as late as September 14th, I was debating which route to take with Fiona...

...and there's the Sudan and Congo, like a great impassable lump over Africa. Both of them haunt me. Which one can I enter to get through to Kampala and peace? I thought the Sudan was the easiest. Now I find I'm wrong. Perhaps it's the Congo after all. The road from Bangassou to the Congolese border at Rutshuru is nearly 1,500 miles long. Unless I can get into a convoy of toughies, I'm sure I won't be able to persuade the border guards to let me through....

There was other paperwork. I worried for a long time about insurance, and asked around a few companies. At no time did I say what car I was driving, mumbling instead about "general inquiries". After Spain, no company was interested. *A carnet de passage* was mandatory, a book of tear-off tickets, one of which is stamped going into a country, the other stamped going out. If I left Alexa in any country, and did not destroy her, then, because my carnet wasn't stamped on exit, I might be liable for any duty to be paid. This document cost me £10, paid through the A.A., to an insurance company, in return for a £200 indemnity.

Driving licenses, both international kinds were easy to obtain from the A.A., at a cost of 10/- for both.

Again, this took time, the more so as I learnt the extent of the paperwork almost casually. The Foreign Office in London, though the ladies there had a helpful manner, was less than helpful in the information I was given...

Overland travellers should not embark on journeys across hazardous regions without first taking expert advice on political conditions, equipment and weather. To ignore this advice is to court disaster... it is inadvisable, being extremely dangerous, to cross from the CAR into the Congo in an attempt to reach East Africa. The influx of Sudanese refugees into the eastern part of the CAR has made it impossible for the local authorities to guarantee the personal safety of travellers...in the Congo the general security situation is poor, particularly in the North East of the country (where I had to go) and travel by car is inadvisable. Road surfaces are very poor, most bridges are unsafe, and the ferries are very unreliable. Travellers would encounter long detours, roadblocks and shortages of food and accommodation...

All this depressed me. I felt I was marching furiously in all directions and ending up where I started.

I collected medical certificates, inoculations against smallpox, typhoid, yellow fever and cholera. When I laid out all the pieces of paper on a table just before I left, I was amazed I had ever managed to shuffle through weary queues, doctors' offices and indifferent embassies to collect them all.

Because of my job as a tour director, and the ease with which I could collect foreign currency, I had expected no trouble with money. My first tour broke even, and I had six weeks between that and my second tour, and only the expenses of the latter to live on. This made finances on the second tour precarious, but by the end of the third tour I was into the black, and I calculated my assets on August 19th as follows:- $300 in Paris in travellers cheques, $250 worth of shares on the New York stock exchange; roughly $400 owed to me in salary and what I had collected in tips.

On the day I was told that another tour director had been given what was to be my last tour, I remember walking down Regent Street and frantically calculating whether I had enough to go or not. My rent was running up, and I had been living and eating on the expectation of more money. Could I go on what I had? There was always the $250 worth of shares to fall back on, but for a long time I was expecting something to come through on a gambling text book I had written, particularly when I heard one publisher was interested in it.

That same day, September 2, I took £5 and wandered into a Soho casino. I had no idea what I would do there, whether I actually considered playing blackjack solidly until I had made what I considered enough for the journey. But I sat there through the afternoon, watching my capital double, start to double again, drop to my original capital, lose a little, gain a little, and finally I lost the lot and walked out dreamily. I did not try that again. It was against my whole idea of gambling anyway, to play when losing hurt so much that a bigger gamble was jeopardised.

In the middle of September, I began writing letters for partial sponsorship. I wrote to three newspapers, the San Francisco *Examiner*, the London *Observer* and the Irish *Independent*. Would they be interested in articles written while on the trip, plus photos? For Alexa, I wrote to Shell and Duckham's, the tyre companies Dunlop and Firestone, and to Sir Donald Stokes, chief of Leyland's, which owned the Austin Motor Company. Following a spate of articles on the Beatles finances, where I read they were sponsoring all sorts of young ideas, I even chanced a letter to them, outlining the risks of the trip and wondering if they might help.

(September 30th), *...but I'm not relying on any of them. Why should anyone come through with anything? Yet all the horses I can back I have backed. It will be easier the more that come up.*

Two did. Duckham's, the oil company, said they would supply my oil needs, as long as I picked up all I wanted in Britain. That saved me money, which I had not got but which needed spending. And the Irish *Independent*, in a lovely letter, said they would take articles as soon as I reached Africa, which was a fair stipulation. They specified 750 words, at £10 an article, two a week, and they would send a draft for accumulated monies to Fiona's address in Joburg.

In time, there were replies from the tyre companies, regretting they no longer gave support to individual endeavours, as I suppose it was too much trouble for too little financial return. Shell also said the same thing, but mentioned in passing the hovercraft trip up the Nile which they *had* backed. The *Observer* didn't reply; nor, of course, did the Beatles. The San Francisco *Examiner*, which I had worked on in 1965, sent me a letter saying they were not interested in travel articles, and added the touching homily that I shouldn't forget my toothbrush. Sir Donald Stokes was angry that I had sent my long letter to his private address, asking if Austin's would check Alexa over before I left, and he sent four lines in reply, saying there was "no commercial interest" in my proposed journey, and wished me the best of luck.

I managed to raise precisely nothing at the beginning of the trip, and watched my dwindling funds, doubtful that I would ever be able to leave. Then, with just the shares left to clear my debts, and the $300 still in Paris... (October 7th)

...a minor miracle seems about to occur. A small publishing company called Rapp and Whiting have accepted my gambling book. Mr. George Rapp said that they wanted to do my book in preference to another, because they liked my style better. I went into a state of apprehensive shock. How much would they pay me? On

what terms? I still have the final version of some chapters to do, on slot machines, two on poker, one on card manipulation and cheating. But what would they pay me? My God, I wanted to know. Would it be enough? I had waited for so long, without hope, that I could not believe this white elephant had finally materialised and turned grey and perceivable...

But George Rapp did not actually come down to terms the next evening. He said he would talk to a lawyer friend and find out whether the situation was going to stabilise at last. The House of Lords was discussing the gambling situation, and while there were rumours that a crack-down was imminent on the hundreds of fringe clubs which were obviously crooked, and concern about a lot of dirty money backing even some outwardly respectable clubs, there was an excellent chance that gambling in a more strictly controlled form would continue legally in Britain. I would have to change my manuscript somewhat to incorporate the new rules, but the bulk of what I had written was valid. That meant a twelfth draft. I didn't care.

For days I waited for news on the book. My friends Mike Winecoff and Jay Jones, fellow would-be writers, got ready to celebrate with me. Then October 15th came and a big end went on Alexa and it all seemed fruitless anyway.

My morale, always a peculiar thing under pressure, had managed to remain at least tangible up to that day. Ever since Fiona had left for South Africa, I had managed, by thinking of her and her marvellous zest for life, to pull myself out of the miseries, whether miseries of frustrated writing or miseries of a frustrated trip out to her. The American, Mike Winecoff, with his slow easy drawl and his openness about his own writing difficulties, drew me in discussions between tours in the early summer. And Jay Jones, another American writer, who always seemed to know where he was going, worked as second anchor on our triangle. There was some authenticity to the three of us and our attempt to live by writing. At moments when Fiona was very far away, Jay and Mike were in the same situation I was, and doing things, so I felt I could do things. If one of us was feeling desperate, it always happened that another was feeling fine. We sucked energy and hope from each other.

But as more difficulties arose, and my marching deadline for leaving marched on, many people who knew about the trip became sceptical about my chances. It was an English scepticism.

"I hear you're going to South Africa in an Austin 7."

"Yes."

"...Really?"

I could never find a justification. It was infuriating. Now I know I should never have tried. One man picked a fight with me, pretending it was a friendly debagging session which fizzled out after five minutes, myself still in possession on my trousers. There was constant, if undefined, resentment at the whole trip.

With this, and my diminishing stock of funds, came the days of Alexa's broken big end and my walk back to Chiswick with Judy. I wandered around Gloucester Road the next day, and in the evening I took a train home to my parents in West Drayton. That night I watched television, something I do when I feel aimless. I told my father Alexa had broken down near Richmond. He did not know officially I was planning to drive down to Johannesburg, though my frantic work on the car when I was supposed to be flying down must have given him a clue. I asked him if he would tow Alexa to the garage at the end of our garden. If it is only one big end gone, I thought, perhaps I will be able to take measurements off the crankshaft, if it isn't damaged, and have a new white-metalled end put on the connecting rod?

I consciously did not think very much further than bringing the car home. Somehow I had to separate each problem, my awful isolation, the money next to gone, the fact that negotiations on the gambling book might drift on for a year (and it all came to nothing in the end), and deal with them one at a time. As a whole, they were almost overwhelming.

 **CHAPTER 3**
Last Stretch

After three days, my father and I drove out as it was getting dark and found Alexa where I had parked her. Despite having no road tax disc showing, she had not been interfered with. I tied the rope to her front axle and to the rear spring of my father's car, and we moved off.

The rope was not very strong and broke continuously. And as Alexa had not been on the road for very long since leaving the garage in Greenwich, the battery was nearly flat. We had an interesting drive back. Every few minutes we stopped and I tied more knots in the rope, so that by the time we reached West Drayton, Alexa was just a few feet from my father's car. I pushed Alexa into our garage and went in to watch television.

Next day I pushed her onto bricks, lifted the engine head, drained the oil, dropped the sump and oil filter, and closed my eyes as pieces of big-end fell on my face. They came from the con-rod on the number one piston, nearest the radiator. The end had shattered completely. I took out the piston and wiped the crankshaft clean, looking for damage.

There appeared to be none.

Though I admitted that I was inexperienced, it looked easy to fix. If I put a micrometer on to the shaft, and found the bore of the big end, surely I could go to an engineer with the con-rod and ask him to white-metal a new big-end to the diameter I asked for? One day, and 17s/6d (87.5 p), was taken up with getting a mechanic from a local garage to come out to the house and micrometer the shaft. Another day I toured around looking for a suitable engineer to do the job. Each evening I sat and watched television.

During those last mornings when I was barely awake, the reality of the situation always hit me. I woke and *knew* I was going to fail, would start questioning why I should even set off. After letting the questions ask themselves, I isolated them, and by dint of argument they would gradually disappear until I was able to get up and carry on collecting spares necessary for the journey. One morning, I realised I must sell the shares; those who owed me money would not pay in time, and those who should come across with money, like the publishers for my gambling book, would be waiting for the gambling situation to stabilise long after I had gone. The shares were my first bid for married responsibility, and I had coveted them more as a symbol than anything else. But they had to go. I wrote to my bank asking them to sell, and to get the money to me quickly.

The white metalling job was soon done, and I picked up the conrod from the engineer and opened up our garage again. Alexa looked very frail with her engine stripped. I was shocked, four days away from her, at her fragility. In that moment, and perhaps three other times on the trip, I saw her as other people did; a small old car, with wire wheels, leaning slightly to the left on a weak front spring, incongruous.

What had made the big end shatter? There were two bolts on the right side of the engine, set into the crankcase, which protected the oil jets. I removed them and pushed a piece of wire down the holes. I had done this before, and thought I had cleaned the jets, but obviously I hadn't. This time, after ten minutes pushing and fiddling, I felt the wire sink suddenly, and knew that both jets had been blocked since the car had been outside Colin's flat. I cleaned the other oil jet, screwed the bolts back in again, and set about putting in the number one piston and assembling the engine.

My father came back from work just as I was finished. He watched while I leaned over the bonnet holding the choke on, and cranked the engine. It started. When I checked the oil pressure it was still off the clock, but after ten minutes warming up, the pressure fell down to around 5 lbs. per sq. inch, just right. I think my father was surprised I could take an engine to pieces and put it together again so that it worked. I felt very pleased. Oil pressure remained good and she ran well.

A couple of days later I began to think of her as a car rather than something delicate and liable to break.

...(Oct 29) I'm still delayed by money. I sold my shares at least 8 days ago, or wrote to the bank then, and I haven't received the money yet. This morning another letter went off, telling them to hurry up. As soon as the money arrives, I can buy all the spares I need, there are lots of them, and within three days of the money arriving, I'm off. It looks like next Tuesday, two weeks late. You had better take a rain cheque for that Christmas dinner, in my name. I don't think I'll make it to you by then, unless I have incredible luck. Once on the road, I will travel as fast as I safely can, but I think it will take 2 ½ months to get to you.

There was trouble with the car two weeks ago. Though her oil pressure was much too high, the mechanics told me it was due to all the special equipment we had put on her, and it was OK, I needn't worry. They were wrong. One of the big ends was starved of oil and shattered. It was a terrible night, full of despair. But I have fixed it, cost £2/10/0 (£2.50), which my parents lent me. Oil pressure is fine now, she runs very well.

My mother gave me some old curtains to line the inside of the roof with, covered in flowers and very jazzy. I bought a roof rack, and packed all my books into a trunk to send to Fiona. All the injections – cholera, typhoid, yellow fever and smallpox – appeared to have taken. I was mildly concerned about malaria tables but left without them. My sister Gerry made me a complete first-aid kit, and bought me a small instamatic camera so I was able to take a few photos on the trip. All my visas had been issued, but I still had nothing for the Congo.

> ...*(Nov 1)... the trip dominates my life. I have bought an extensive tool kit, and feel myself capable of mending anything but a complete write-off. There will be some difficult moments, particularly in the desert, but if I don't rush I will get through safely. The cooling system is fine now, and with the addition of a condenser all those worries your friends have that the radiator might blow are groundless. I feel confident, not over-confident, I hope, but just good that I can see how the car works and feel that I can fix most things. I wish the money were here. I want to set off so badly that I am suffering from terrible blues which last for hours, and which I cannot shake off. These days are gutted, worth nothing, but I must wait. It won't be long, I hope...*

I made attempts to push the gambling book for a sale, without success (I must admit I had been so overjoyed that it might be published that I was afraid to do anything that might put George Rapp off). Then a literary agent, Hope Leresche of Leresche and Steele, asked to see me on the strength of a play I had written in Ireland on casino gambling, called *The Highroller.* Mrs Leresche liked the play, and we signed a contract so that she would market it for me. I gave her all my other stuff, a small novel, some short stories, responsibility for the gambling textbook manuscript, and told her that the *Irish Independent* was taking articles from me on a trip through Africa, and was there a chance they could be syndicated? Everything began to move.

On November 6, $230, the money from the sale of shares arrived. I was infused with energy. That evening I paid off debts; Alexa MacPherson for ten week's back rent, Judy Entwistle for some money which she had lent me, and my parents for putting up the money for repair work. My father now accepted the fact that I was going. I think he saw the same chance in the trip that I did. As my mother had always been an incurable romantic, which had made my attempt at being a writer easier to live with, she threw herself immediately into organising all those things – clothes, toothpaste, washing flannels, dishcloths, towels, sleeping bags – which mothers claim as their prerogative.

Next day, Thursday, I spent in town, talking to Mrs. Leresche, buying spare parts, and visiting the garage in Greenwich one more time to have a drink with Brian and Malcolm. They tuned the engine for me on their flashing complicated machine, tightened down the last nuts and bolts, then retired to our pub across the road to drink and talk about how I would pay them. Their bill, incredibly, came to £10, which I gave them. Though I had discovered some of the mistakes on the car, both men had gone to enormous trouble in helping me at a time when others were full of words and little else. If they had not helped, I certainly would not have been able to leave.

The weekend was taken up looking for petrol cans, which I found on Monday. Valentine's Paints in West Drayton gave me as many old five-gallon paint cans as I wanted, with snap-down tops, and a sealer. I took five, four for petrol and one for water. Duckham's sent eight gallons of their 20-50 oil, plus grease and other little oddments. I left a busy house, my mother sewing, my sister Gerry adding to my medical kit, my father buying ham and cheese and crackers for a daily and long-range food supply, and drove around to say goodbye to people. The farewell to Mike and his wife Susan was particularly poignant. I would soon be in Africa, Jay was probably going to marry his girlfriend Fran and leave for Canada; that left Mike in England to face the winter on his houseboat, washing dishes to eat, and trying to write.

I took Judy out to dinner on Monday night. We talked about my trip, her wanting to go to South America, and the agony Mark Lerminier, a friend of the Campbells must have caused Fiona by gossiping about us to her parents. I said that just as long as I set off, Fiona would know everything was fine, and Judy, after some discussion about whether she should write to Fiona, agreed.

All of Tuesday, I packed equipment into the car. In spite of all my work, and because of money trouble, much less was done to Alexa than I had originally planned. Instead of special springs to heighten the ground clearance, I had bought one spare rear spring and one spare front one, but kept them for emergencies. As I was again running short of money, I had not bought the spare half-shaft I thought I might need. I had meant to buy a spare piston but, fatally, I didn't. Everything was packed on to the back seat, instead of into lockers, which I had originally envisioned. A new clutch had been put into the car. An SU type replaced the Zenith carburettor, so I was able to fit an air filter from a mini-Cooper, which wasn't really effective against sand. I didn't get a water-cooled sump. The car was re-wired, but I never did get the fuel gauge to work, and with large headlamps on the wings, I believe I over-strained both the battery and the wings themselves.

I had tried the tyre companies for help, with no success. Instead of a complete set of new 17 x 4 ½ inch tyres, plus a spare set of four, as I had hoped, I left with six complete wheels I had picked up second hand, and not even a spare inner-tube. Three tyres were remoulds, including one that was completely bald and which amazed me later because it punctured only once. The other three tyres had been used, but not much. I remembered in Spain to buy a puncture kit.

As for the water condenser I had mentioned so assiduously in letters to reassure Fiona. I *had* bought the radiator cap without a pressure spring, necessary to fit the condenser, but again, nothing else. I expected to rig up something before I reached the desert.

Colin Hunter gave me a large jack that I could not fit under the car unless I dug a hole and pushed the car over the hole. Brian and Malcolm gave me another, again too large, a defective hydraulic jack that packed up completely in central Africa, but which I sold for a fine price. I had a set of six BS spanners, a set of six AF, plus three screwdrivers, a pair of pliers, tappet spanners, a tyre pressure gauge (soon lost), and various pieces of wire. So much for my vaunted "complete tool set".

For spares, aside from the two springs, I took two complete sets of spark plugs, one set of points, a condenser, two spare valves, three complete sets of gaskets, two fan-belts (one of which turned out to be too big, but which mercifully I was able to exchange in Nigeria), and some nuts and bolts.

Alexa had a new battery, her radiator had been reconditioned, brake linings renewed (though she still failed the M.o.T. test on brakes), and a new canvas roof in four layers was nailed and screwed to the body.

By 5 o'clock on Tuesday evening, November 12, 1968, I was satisfied with the packing of the petrol cans on the back seat, and drove off to fill them. Petrol is more expensive in France than Britain. It was dark when I returned, and my father was going off on night shift as an air traffic controller at London Heathrow Airport. We said goodbye as we always did on other occasions when I had left home, rather casually, talking about small things. I found I had not enough money to get to Paris that morning, where $300 was waiting for me, and he had given me another £15. Then my mother gave me tea and we spent the evening checking over lists of clothing, toilet articles, and the contents of both food boxes. Once I phoned Judy and said goodbye. I expected Colin Hunter to phone, but he didn't. I made periodic trips across the garden, muttering to myself, to arrange everything handily.

Finally, at 10 o'clock the car was packed, with only Brunehilde the typewriter to go in. I sat down and wrote an article for the *Irish Independent*. It was published, I heard later, on November 19th, with a cutaway of a Cortina which had crossed Africa, showing all the extensive modifications necessary for a car to survive the journey, laughable besides my amateur efforts.

In 700 words I attempted to summarise all the preparations and pitfalls in bringing the car into shape for the journey. Though I had promised a 2,000-mile test run through Scotland before I left, I had not the money to try it. I was setting off anyway, with perhaps a little bravado, and trusting to hard work and luck to succeed. Now, looking at the article, it is not difficult to recapture my surroundings as I wrote it; cars going by on the nearby M4, a quiet dining-room, muffled sounds of television next door, all the work behind me at last and just a bare realisation that in the morning I would be up at 5 o'clock for breakfast and on the road to Dover before dawn.

I finished the article, put it in an envelope, ran across the street to post it, and went into the sitting room to say goodnight to my sister and mother. Then I went up to bed and fell asleep almost at once.

 **CHAPTER 4**
Europe

November 13th - 23rd, 30220 - 31790, mileage covered 1,570 miles.

My mother woke me at 5 o'clock in the morning. She made breakfast and packed sandwiches while I started the car's engine, checking over my luggage while it warmed up. After a quick meal, I backed Alexa out of the garage, waved to my mother shivering in her blue housecoat and drove up to the M4, half a mile from the house.

There were comparatively few cars on the road, and I had little difficulty getting through London and on to the Dover Road. I felt very strange, laughing suddenly four or five times, terribly aware of what was happening, a kind of gigantic freedom. Formalities at the 10 o'clock ferry in Dover were minimal; within five minutes of arriving I drove on to the boat and parked the car.

Mileage on the clock when I left home was 30,220. With the car's history this probably meant it had gone around only once in 32 years, a total of 130,220 miles, still with the original engine. She ran beautifully, despite the huge load.

The crossing was uneventful. I talked to a couple of American tourists without mentioning the trip, for they would not have understood. From experience in Europe during the past summer, I was able to suggest places for them to visit. After landing at Boulogne I bought insurance for the car, and was quickly on the road that took me through Montreuil-Sur-Mer, Abbeville and Beauvais to Paris. That night I slept on the floor of a friend's flat. Next morning at 10 o'clock I went to the American Express building on Rue Scribe and picked up $300 in traveller's cheques. I was now self-sufficient.

On the way out of Paris on the N20, on a crisp autumn day, with a clear blue sky, smoke began pouring into the cabin. I stopped and opened the bonnet, and discovered it came from under the exhaust manifold. I removed the manifold, thinking the gasket had blown, and put in a new gasket. Later in the day more smoke drifted in from the engine. I suspected a valve was blowing, but again it stopped so I stopped worrying. In all, 160 miles were covered; I camped in a small village called Vatan.

That night I sat in my tent, wind lifting the flaps, with a torch in my mouth and my typewriter on an empty petrol can and wrote to Fiona. I told her I felt great gouts of civilisation clinging to me, and was preparing to slough them off. Outside, the leaves rustled softly. People walked by on the road twenty yards away, curious about the car and someone camping this late in the season. No one came over.

On the third day, too rushed to re-grind valves, I ate and drove on quickly, through Chateauroux, Limoges, Thiviers, 185 miles to a camping site at Pont-St. Mametz. It was a beautiful place, with quiet woods, and a green valley covered with a slight mist, quite deserted. After setting up camp, I was visited by the *patron*, a Count Guy de Lauriere, who asked me to have dinner with him. We ate at a nearby restaurant. Guy was about 40 years old, with a thin sad face, and over his food he told me what he thought of the Paris manifestations. I revelled in the food and talked my head off, stammering a disagreement in poor French.

I spent all the next morning removing the valves and grinding them in again, and de-coked the engine; it was, strangely, coked up. Though I was on the road as late as 1.45 p.m., I managed to drive 114 miles through Bergerac and Casteljaloux to Mont-de-Marsan before dusk. But I was in too much of a hurry, and nearly crashed. Reaching for a cigarette going into a bend, I misjudged the curve, and the car bounced up a grassy bank, tilted alarmingly, swayed and rolled back down again. It was a great relief to know that the suspension was strong enough to take the shock, but I resolved to be more careful; that would have been an absurd way to end the trip.

That evening, November 16th, I sat in a café and collected impressions and thoughts. It was almost the first time I had stopped and thought since receiving my money from shares ten days beforehand. The impressions were vivid in my head, having been turned over and over for ten or twenty miles after I had seen them.

... The old hag at Chateauroux hanging the tattered bodies of dead rabbits from a hook through their dead throats, so they swung in the cold morning wind.

... My thickness, full of the days after tomorrow, still thinking of banks, running water and people I knew. I had to kick myself to realise they will not be where I was going.

...If I kept my patience, I would get through Spain and Morocco to Algiers, safely. But where would I sleep? I had been told there were camping sites. Algiers was the marker for the second stage, probably the most difficult, crossing the Sahara. As long as there were no checkpoints, I should reach In Salah without some bureaucrat telling me to go home, as my car was not suitable. There, though, will be the Commandant. How high he bulked in my daydreams! I saw myself arguing with him, as reasonable men, as *sportifs*, as madmen, as youth and age. Each time he was moved by my arguments to allow me to continue, despite regulations governing traffic across the desert. The scene was always the same. I drive off south looking cheerful but determined. He waves, with a nearly cynical smile, and keeps a watch out for me on the Trans-Sahara radio. Perhaps he even bets with his friends that I get across. In my daydreams, after terrible trials, I do, and celebrate Christmas in Kano, Nigeria. But these dreams aside, providing I get across (and I was determined), the run down to the Congo through the Cameroons, Chad, and the Central African Republic should be fairly straightforward. There was a question mark against each country, I did not know them at all, but they seemed fine. I could not worry about these countries because I was worrying too much about the Congo. Somewhere, from someone, it had filtered through to me that they issued 8-day transit visas on the border, and *they could not be extended.* I had to cover 1,400 miles in that time, though the days would be much longer than they were at present. I had glucose tablets. I bet the other drivers used Benzedrine. I wondered if I could get some? I could sleep in Uganda, for days even, in relief. From Uganda to Johannesburg was too sweet to think about. It almost seemed academic. I knew how slim my chances were.

...How good food tasted when cooked in the open!

...A sign saying CONDOM 80 kms. It seemed a long way to go.

...There was a tiny girl in a blue dress playing table-football in the bar at Mont-de-Marsan. She was totally absorbed, but what was fascinating was her size and her prettiness. Pert, short glossy black hair, occasional Gauloise like a cigar in her mouth, tiny breasts (what size bra?); all the boys clustered round her.

On November 17th, I drove through Biarritz and into Spain. It was lashing rain. I tried to buy insurance, but the office on the border was closed. From then on I did not worry about it. I had never been to Spain before, but it was Hemingway country, an author with whom I had a passionate love/hate relationship. I passed a signpost to Pamplona, and realised I had been on the road taken by Jake Barnes in *The Sun Also Rises*, after the bull-fighting, when Brett has left with her matador, and Barnes went to Biarritz and cooled his frustration by swimming.

On reaching Puerto La Brujla, 3250 feet high, the country sombre and purple in the evening light, I wondered how many people had died there this century for plain political reasons. An American friend called Leslie Woolf Hedley had been thrown off a boat going to the Spanish Civil War – he was 15 at the time. What was it here that drew him into politics at that age? As each old man I passed I wondered, what side had he been on? What blood had he seen? How many villages raped and re-raped? What did it matter anyway, as long as you survived?

In Burgos, staying at a skid-row hotel, probably used as a casual whorehouse, with voices and footsteps at night, I was pleased to have covered 237 miles in a day, but staggered with exhaustion. I took a bath, and rested, there beginning a daydream that occurred frequently until I met Fiona again. In it, I arrived in South Africa, and she wasn't there, or she had married someone else, tired of waiting for me, or she did not even know me. In the dream I went to great lengths in producing her letters and waving them in front of her. Though Fiona was kind, and very sorry, she kept saying, "But who are you?" and the whole thing started again, occurring and re-occurring.

Though roads varied greatly from province to province, they were gradually getting worse. I spent an apprehensive half day in a hotel in Madrid, expecting something magical to happen for no reason I could think of, except perhaps Hemingway's play *The Fifth Column;* every time the lights flickered, I imagined gunfire, that the fascists were coming. Instead, there were berserk drivers who constantly honked their horns in waves from each red traffic light, and obvious keen Americans, and a bank which wouldn't change my traveller's cheques.

Five Americans and one Englishman were staying overnight at my hotel. They talked before dinner, while I sat in a corner listening, pretending to read an old magazine. I wanted to join in but felt I shouldn't, as I would be cheating on an ethical equation. With the niceties of English speech, the silences, starts and stops, small murmurs of places visited, the American election, violence, ex-patriotism, I felt clumsy and rather lonely.

I felt detached anyway in big cities, cut off from reality. Down on the street Alexa was just an old car, the potential victim of any whim of an urchin or a policeman. She was something to laugh at, as happened frequently in Spain. Only when camping did I feel at ease, with her next to the tent, primed and ready for the mornings, supplier of all I needed. If she broke down I could fix her, there in the open, away from other eyes.

One more image added to my collection, on the way into Madrid. I rounded a bend in the hills and there, silhouetted against the sky, were three men stringing telephone wire on two poles. The men were draped over crosspieces, and for a shocking moment they seemed to assume the peculiar postures of agony of men nailed on a cross. I had to shake my head to destroy the image.

A new day's record, 262 miles, clocked on the 20th. In the week since leaving home, I had driven 1,079 miles, and aside from smoke in the cabin (now ceased), without mechanical trouble. My route took me through Valdepenas, up an immense hill to Las Correderas, then Cordoba, and on into the night another 44 miles. Again, I stayed in a guesthouse, paying precious money for food I should have cooked myself more cheaply, and all because I neglected to fill my water tank.

Finally, November 21st, after the worst tarmac I had seen, on route N340, I drove into Algeciras and saw the bulk of Gibraltar across the bay. There was a camping site a mile out of town. When I drove in and parked and looked around, I was delighted to find myself in the company of a number of mad souls.

I had thought I would be lonely on the trip, and was prepared for it. Madrid was the beginning, I felt, of a long dive into solitude. There was a great deal to think about, sitting each day driving, no one to talk to, and I was always watching the road, and digesting information on routes, or even enjoying the scenery. But at night it was another thing, as Jake Barnes said. Sitting by a Primus stove, wind flapping the tent, a hundred thousand stars bright in a country sky, then the awful awareness of being alone came on me. A good way to fight this, I found, was to emphasise small things; take time setting cutlery on a plank as if it was a dinner table, pause over coffee, lay out the site with everything near me, check tyres fussily, Alexa's oil, water, petrol, wash up immediately after the dinner cigarette, and so on.

Now, with Africa across the straits, I found all the other people who were making the journey overland to South Africa. It was as if Spain had funnelled them into a narrow spout at this one camping site. There were to be some surprises for me.

As I was setting up camp, a Swiss called Robert Auberson came over from his magnificent tent where he had been sitting like the pukka sahib in the Camp coffee label. He spoke no English, and over coffee, using my slow and mangled French, I asked him where he was going. He pointed to his car where a map of Africa was painted on the door, and said he was going to tour the entire coast. I told him I was going to South Africa, a point I had been very shy about since I arrived in Europe. He looked at Alexa and shrugged.

Robert was an orphan, about 30 years old, wiry build, going prematurely bald. He made his living officially as a photographer, bumming around Africa in his Citroen 2CV (with a 3CV engine) looking for likely situations to photograph, or if he could, to get in on them and make himself a profit. His tent was full of supplies; cheap sunglasses, lighters, medical equipment of every description, beads, cloth, anything small and Western which would make good currency to trade with the natives. He told me he had £1,000 invested in these goods. I heard later that in Tamanrasset, he brought out a huge trunk from his car and waited for Arabs to cluster around him. Then for five hours, sometimes pulling goods quickly from the trunk and flashing them in front of the crowd, other times pretending disgust at slow sale and packing everything away, making as if to leave, he bartered with them. Perhaps a few knives, some gold ornaments, food and drink. Whatever, Robert was supremely confident he would leave Africa richer than when he arrived.

He told me he had bought his car for the equivalent of £15, in a deal so complicated I couldn't follow it. He was waiting for money from a photographic agency, but I heard later that having secretly contacted another agency to distribute his photographs, and been found out, Robert lost them both. He went to Africa with his own money, hoping to find a profitable situation.

Then an Englishman, Tom Pearson, came over with two of his four sons. He was bound for Kenya, he said, later admitting it was South Africa, but thinking it bad policy to tell people in Black Africa where he was really going ... as if they didn't know. A huge and tough-looking ex-army 10 tonner contained all his family's possessions. When I walked over to look, it appeared to have been there for months. Tom and his family, including a very shy wife, had left England the year before, and driven across Europe. Tom earned money as a mechanic. He was very good, and his sons were learning from him. As soon as the sand settled on the Hoggar Trail across the Sahara, he said he and his family would be off. It was only much later I thought he was kidding, even himself. They all had a marvellously easy life, driving south in winter, and back north in summer, picking up jobs for a season, then moving off. Why risk Africa?

Robert told me that six English Landrovers. grossly over-loaded with supplies and carrying 33 people, had left for Morocco five hours before I arrived. He was very scathing about their chances of getting across the desert, with good reason, as I learned later. I determined to catch them if I could, but decided to rest for two days at the camp site, clean the car, find out why it was using so much petrol (only 35 m.p.g. on a run), and write letters and articles.

The following morning I noticed a battered yellow van with five incredibly scruffy men bustling around it. I talked to two of them. They said they were also going to South Africa, but they were surly and looked like they wanted a fight, so we didn't talk much. There was a big drunken

quarrel that night, and next day only four scruffs were left,
the other having stormed off and returned to England. The
survivors packed their tent, heaved their van around the site
to start it – the starter motor didn't work then, or later –
jumped payment for camping, and took a boat across to
Africa. They had no spares, two maps, a rope, a promise of
petrol cans, and the grave doubts of the rest of us. Their
story, as I was to hear it later, was an interesting one.

What struck me about all these people was how little
trouble they had taken to find out about driving in Africa. I
had more information about routes, though well out of date,
than all of them, including Robert. Rumours spread
insidiously. Tom was worried about the Arabs slitting his
family's throats. Robert carried at least two guns; a rifle and
a revolver, plus the protection of a dog, Zeta, which didn't
like black people. The scruffs knew they had to cross the
Sahara, but had planned no route, expecting to follow
signposts. And even the Landrover convoy, which I met in
Algiers, originally planned to drive through the Sudan,
which in the last six years had had an idiot's politics and was
extremely dangerous. Then there were the numerous small
things one must know, like the last town to buy petrol, or the
last town with a bank (I missed that one, and had to go back),
or water holes and the state of the water; everyone seemed
prepared to just chance it. I felt a positive veteran with all my
painfully acquired knowledge, and shared it with them,
which at least stopped any open sarcasm about my own
chances of getting through.

Tom tuned Alexa's engine for thirty shillings (£1.50). He
said the mixture was set far too rich, and he showed me how
to set it myself. He also de-coked the engine again, and
rigged up an old shampoo bottle and a rubber pipe as a
condenser for the radiator. It was very effective, and saved
me vital pints of water. Tom also greased all the points,
changed the oil, and generally serviced the car. I was
grateful, and aside from payment, I gave his family porridge
for one breakfast; they had not eaten it in a year.

One of Tom's sons helped me buy the last pieces of

equipment I needed; two small rolls of chicken netting, used as sand-mats; a hundred feet of tough nylon rope, a hurricane lamp, puncture outfit, spares, paraffin, spare prickers for the Primus, and some torch batteries saved by those crooks of shopkeepers to sell to tourists, which last five minutes only before fading. With the car cleaned, equipment packed securely, a good meal, and the feeling which others reflected that I could possibly succeed, I felt in excellent spirits.

On the night of 22nd November, three South Africans arrived in a minibus; Willy, Henri and a girl called Joy, with an English hitchhiker called Ian. I sat in their car to type the *Irish Independent* article. They nearly died laughing at Alexa, but after a few drinks, felt that if I was going to attempt to drive overland to their country, they should try, too. They were Afrikaners, the first I had met, tremendously interested in my experiences in Paris that May (as tour guide to some Americans – we obviously became involved in the manifestations there), and full of sympathy for the students.

When I innocently asked them about South Africa, they assured me that demonstrators had a hard time from the police, because they were mostly "communist infiltrated". South Africa was a unique country, they asserted ("but it's a beautiful place, man"), and I would have to live there and see the conditions to understand their point of view. The Government had to act the way it did for the general good and a few misguided people might unfortunately get hurt.

The subject came back to their projected overland drive again. They said they would beat me down there despite setting off after me. Henri was worried about the Blacks, whom he called "'kaffirs" and was going to buy a .45 pistol and shoot his way through border posts. I did not think this would be necessary, but he said I would find out soon, and I did not know Africans. After I left, they decided they would not be able to make the trip anyway, because of possible trouble with visas, and they carried on being tourists in Europe.

 # CHAPTER 5
Morocco

November 23rd - 25th, 31790 - 32216 (426 miles)
1570 to 1996 miles from London

Throughout Africa I used a motoring guidebook produced in 1960 by the Automobile Association, and even though it was 8 years old and the decolonisation movement was in full cry, it still told a vestige of the truth. It said that Morocco was a kingdom of 11 million, with a capital in Rabat, and its language was Arabic. The climate was Mediterranean, but it was colder in the mountain regions. The Berber population earned its living mostly by agriculture, but phosphate represented 20% of its exports. It had well-developed all-weather roads between the main centres, and travellers should contact the Royal Moroccan Automobile Club in Rabat, or the Touring Club du Maroc in Casablance if they wanted more details.

The route I had to take, along the coast from the Spanish enclave of Ceuta towards Oran in Algeria, was described as tarred throughout, in good condition. It was hilly and sinuous with fine views of the sea and mountains, and numerous villages with plentiful petrol.

November 23rd, camped 40 miles south of Tangiers

Sitting under a whirl of stars in the black sky. Behind me, having covered 118 miles today, streetlights in the town of Chechaoueh stretch to a corner in the road. My tent is on my left, the car on the right, and beyond the car, the coast road to Algiers. I am typing by hurricane lamplight. A cat prowls round the tent, looking at me. Further into the darkness, a dog shifts on its haunches, waiting until I sleep to sniff around for scraps. There are none; I was hungry, too.

I said goodbye to all the camping site madmen today and rode across the Straits of Gibraltar on a boat called the *Virgin of Spain*. There was a strong sea swell, so the cars had to be roped together. I was nearly sick, but it passed. In Ceuta, I bought 25 gallons of petrol, enough to get past Algiers, at 6 pesetas to the litre; that's about three shillings and fourpence a gallon (4.5p/litre). Alexa carries the weight well.

Leaving town, I lost my way. Roads were badly signposted. I managed only sixty real miles before camping. There was a puncture on the rear offside wheel at 6.30, which, with my oversize jacks, was a perfect bastard to fix. It took an hour to change wheels. The first blot on the car's record.

In the night, dogs barked continuously. The sound carried for miles. Cars were very rare. It was quiet enough for the crickets to make a great noise. Stray thoughts took a long time to struggle into cognition. I drove too fast; there was no need to hurry. I would be at the beginning of the Sahara next week. If I was to succeed in getting across, I had to be patient. But whenever the road was flat and straight for miles, I found myself up around 40 mph, with punch still in the car, and my foot impatient to push on.

Alexa fascinated everyone, who became too interested for my peace of mind. I dared not leave her a moment. Once, four policemen stepped out into the road and stopped me. There was nothing wrong. They just wanted to know the year the car was built, and how much it cost. I told the truth in answer to the first question, 1937, but lied to the second, saying "oh, about eight hundred dollars American". They asked why, and I said the car was "très rare". They whistled, listened to the engine, complimented me, and drove on smiling. I had to prepare myself for every eventuality. If the car did break down, and could not be fixed, even if I mortgaged my soul in the attempt, then I would get a good price for it. But thinking onto the typewriter with no one to list all the dangers ahead and my nightmares and sleep an hour away, I thought I would make it.

Urchins in Morocco were very forward. I stopped to ask the way once, and talked to a young boy who spoke little French. He couldn't tell me where a camping site was, but was well able to reel off a plea for dollars, which said volumes for the tourist trade in his country. And whatever road I drove on, no matter how deserted it looked, youngsters were always popping up with handfuls of what looked like grass and waving violently for me to stop and buy. In sixty miles, I had come near to running down three of these young salesmen.

It was late now. The moon, a thin clipping of fingernail, which gave a gentle aura to the mountains, had gone for the night. Up at 2,000 feet the air was clear. Time for long thought.

Fiona, in South Africa, the girl I was driving to marry, I thought about her a great deal. Some people asked me whether, so far, I had been desperate enough to chuck it in, particularly when no one gave me a hope of getting through. Of course, there had been no real difficulties yet. But whenever they appeared to crop up, like once in Spain, when I started the car and it sounded like another big-end had gone (fuel/air mixture was too rich), the thought of crawling into Johannesburg with a kitbag was so immediately depressing that I felt I was able, anyway, to deal with a broken big end in a country where I could not speak a word of the language. I wondered whether other people, who made long journeys on their own, rated shame of failure high on their incentives?

My back ached. I was starting to get cold. Tomorrow I had to mend the puncture and make sure I ate a good meal. North

Africa had enough food stores to enable me to buy food daily. It would be foolish to cut into my tinned supplies. I would certainly need them later, in the desert.

Men walked by occasionally. Typing in the open air, with a small lamp, one felt very vulnerable. I stopped whenever I heard anyone, and watched them pass. Probably over-cautious.

24th November, camped in a rocky wadi 3 miles past Al Hoceima, after driving 139 miles in mountainous country

It was hot today, the first time. Crawling out of the tent to set up my first cup of coffee, I felt the South wind off the desert. Three urchins hovered around the car while I made coffee and scratched my hair. They were poor, in rags, with quick smiles, begging cigarettes and saying "pour mon pere, c'est vrai". Instead of being for their fathers, the cigarettes were for themselves. A man went by on a donkey, his robes flowing, looking like a lord, and, by a hand grasped around the donkey's tail, his wife followed, running and stumbling to keep up. I ate, washed, shaved, left the spare tyre to be mended later, and drove away, after paying the urchins' persistence with a cigarette apiece. One youngster with a racking smoker's cough had come to join three five-year olds hanging around the car. They all waited for cigarettes, but the newcomer was impatient. He had to have his quickly; after all, he was eight years old. Giving them cigarettes was part of the ethical equations again, like the old payment to the gods.

One of the small goals was catching the convoy of six Landrovers, which I had heard about at the camping site. Though they left three days ahead of me, I thought that when I reached Morocco I might hear of their recent passing. Six cars must always travel slower than one. At about noon today, I had run out of petrol, after 160 miles on five gallons, most of the time in second gear, which is pretty good. As I was filling the tank from one of my cans, I heard a loud roaring noise, and three motorcycles drew up, with

five wild-looking cowboys on them. The conversation went
something like this:-
    "Hello" – (me startled)
    "Hi, there! Where're you going?"
    "South Africa."
    "In that? Hey, man another one. We're going there too."
    "On those?"
    "That's right!"
    "Which way?"
    "Through the Sudan. Which way are you going?"
    "Across the Sahara," (me, confidently). "It's the only way."
    "You sure?"
    "Have you got a route?"
    "No. We only decided three days ago. We've got to buy
maps and things yet."
    Introductions followed. Three were Canadian, two were
British. We decided to camp together if one didn't
outdistance the other.
    The Cowboys had met the Landrover convoy the previous
day. I had wondered how far ahead they were. Three hours
later I met the last Landrover, the sweeper, on the side of the
mountain. The road curved up and up to five and half
thousand feet, and down the other side, on one of the hills,
the motorcycle Cowboys had stopped to talk to the driver of
the sweeper. I almost crashed into them, for my brakes
nearly failed through over-heating.
    The Landrover driver was English, with a young girl,
resting the car. Later, I met another, the driver tired, rather
shocked-looking. It was curious to hear they were not
certain of a lot of things, routes, visas, and road conditions.
Each of them had paid a man called Tim Bailey £200 to
make the trip. Tomorrow I hope to catch him and find out
what's what. Secretly, I would be tickled pink to hand out
information, and I would love to pass the lot and show them
the way. The convoy was going slow enough, so we would
see what happened.
    That night at our small camp, in the half-light of a
hurricane lamp and candle, the motorcyclists and I discussed

the trip. Their idea came in the most peculiar way. It started with an English mechanic called Ian, the quietest of the bunch, setting out from England with a friend, in a psychedelic motorbike and sidecar, bound for South Africa. The friend found a lot of excuses in Spain to stop, and when Ian reached Tangiers the friend opted out. Ian did not want to continue on his own, so he waited around for a few days, with a "For Sale" notice on the bike, but in half a mind to continue.

Now Peter, a young bearded English mechanic, and Paul Stott, a 19 year-old Canadian college dropout, came into the picture. Paul was blowing his mind in Tangiers after a summer of bumming around Europe. He had apparently been high for four days. Peter found him wandering the streets, broke and happy. Peter, in a mad gallop to see the world after a five-year mechanical engineering apprenticeship, persuaded Paul to come down from his druggy high, and they both went off to Gibraltar and found Ian.

"Want to go to South Africa?" said Ian.

"Why not?" said Peter and Paul.

Another Canadian, a young blond-haired fellow called Brian, pitched up; he had known Paul in other parts of Europe. Brian was co-opted, went out and found a motor-bike for sale at $30 by an American who had chickened out of the Sahara crossing, and the four of them set off for the ferry.

On the way, they met another Canadian, Bruce, who was wandering Europe on a motorbike, sending his money from one American Express office to another, and he was roped in too. They had been going three days when I met them.

Now Ian was asleep, and Bruce was worrying where to send his money next. Paul had been elected leader, and I managed to persuade them to cross the Sahara Desert, instead of going by way of the Sudan. From my AA list, they had information on what equipment they would need, which they could buy tomorrow. Brian was very jumpy, and looked to Paul for leadership. He seemed high-strung, a natural pot head, and admitted that each country he had visited he headed straight for the potheads to orientate himself. He felt that if he made it across the Sahara, he would find out just what he was made of. All of us felt that.

I was becoming aware of a sort of fraternity of the roads. We were told where someone else was every day, who was going to cross which trail across the desert. In the next week, I expected to add others, so that by the time I reached the desert itself, I would be fitted into a convoy strung out over hundreds of miles. The four Scruffs who left the camp without paying must be hundreds of miles from here now, going strong the last time Paul saw them. I would like to catch them before Algiers.

My tyre fixed, I was whole again.

On November 25th, the Cowboys rushed in all directions to buy supplies. There was a great trauma about cutting their hair, which Paul insisted on, as they had heard the Algerians are very neurotic about long hair. In the end, Paul cut off his side-burns, which they all knew he was very proud of, and then it was fine.

The Scruffs turned up and said hello. Apparently, I had passed their camping site the previous day. After talking for two minutes, there was consternation and they rushed off the way they had come to pick up their starting handle, which they had left behind. I did not see them again, and left early, expecting the Cowboys to catch me before Algiers.

I drove all day, with hardly a stop, on the look out for the Landrovers, and watching my rear-view mirror for the Cowboys, without seeing either. In all, I covered 199 miles in the day, passing into Algeria as the sun went down. My comment in my ragged notebook went "No trouble at border, but the Algerian fellow wanted to eat and fool around with his mates before clearing me through, so I had to wait half an hour". I did not know he had not eaten all day, and would fast during the daytime forty days of the feast of Ramadan. But I did learn that the Landrovers had passed through an hour and a half ahead of me, so I drove in the dark until 7 o'clock, looking vainly for their camp. I was so shattered that night I set up tent, ate, and fell asleep immediately.

CHAPTER 6
Algeria

The AA guide said of Algeria that it was a republic (after a long and bloody war to throw the French out) of 10.5 million people, its capital being Algiers. Its normal language was Arabic, but French was fairly common. Algeria's climate was Mediterranean in the north, but the southern part had desert conditions with irregular and infrequent rain. Seven eights of the country was desert, the Sahara, but the coastal strip was fertile (wine growing), and there was high oil production in the south-east. Algeria also had iron ore and natural gas deposits. Tourists were attracted to the coastal resorts, and the roads along the coast were very good.

The road I took along the coast from Oran to Algiers was in good condition, tarred throughout, hilly and sinuous with fine views of the sea and mountains. Heading south towards Laghouat I could still enjoy driving on tarred surfaces, but faced two mountain ranges in the Atlas chain, passing through Djelfa at the highest point, 3,757 feet above sea level.

November 25 to December 12, 32,216 - 34,261 (2,045 miles) 1,996 miles from London

A Typical Day...

Usually, I wake at dawn. I have the tent closed, and there has been no rain, so I'm dry. But my sleeping bag is not up to the cold nights, and I shift around at first, trying to get warm. The night before, I had filled the kettle and the Primus stove, and put them on a wooden board next to the sleeping bag. Still in the bag, and struggling, I shift the stove out, light it, put the kettle on it and stare at it all, amazed at my energy. That is my first coherent thought, chasing the dregs of dreams that must make me talk a lot out loud when I'm asleep.

Next, a cigarette, a habit I have picked up in the last two weeks, smoking before breakfast. I check the zipped closed pocket of my fur-lined jacket, which is draped over the sleeping bag, to see if my lighter is there. It is the fourth most valuable thing I had after the car, my travellers' cheques and the typewriter.

Soon, the kettle steams, and I hop outside, putting on sandals or cowboy boots, depending on the weather. I have baths periodically; last time was six days ago. I sleep in my clothes, leaving off enough to put on in the morning to keep me warm. Quickly, not thinking, I mix porridge and hot water, and some milk from the powder I have brought, and with both coffee and porridge inside me, I feel better. I may have some hardboiled eggs if I manage to buy any the day before.

With my stomach temporally satisfied, I turn to Alexa, the car. I check the oil, water, and battery, filling where I need to. The more miles we travel, the less she needs each day. When the essentials are taken care of, I start her up, take off choke as soon as possible, screw up the accelerator to run the engine moderately fast, and leave her for half an hour while I wash, shave, clean my teeth, and break camp.

The car has to be re-packed. Considering all the equipment I have brought, settling it correctly is surprisingly easy. A full petrol can comes out of the line on the back seat and is replaced by the empty petrol can of yesterday. This is to make it easy to fill up, as I have to, at least once a day. The tent, groundsheet, and sleeping bag are pushed into one sack, and this is hammered and punched under the back window, stabilising the water can on one side and the day's full petrol can on the other. My day-to-day food box also fits between these cans, on a wooden board. The typewriter, a huge Olympia 9 made in 1947, is wrapped in a plastic bag on the seat next to me, and the long-range food box plus the coffee odds-and-ends bucket, fit onto the floor in front of it. My clothes are in a case on the roof, except for shirts and underwear, which are pressed in another case between the back of my seat and the line of petrol cans. Other things, like oil, frying pan, kettle, hurricane lamp, tea-pot, umbrella (for impressing border guards, along with a three-piece check suit and good shoes) etc, fit into gaps here and there. I drape the fur jacket over the typewriter, and my active map goes on top of that.

I check the tyres by kicking them, and I know now how they should look. Nevertheless, I order myself to check the pressures at least once a day. I pump the back tyres to 26 lbs./ sq. inch, the front to 22 lbs. / sq. inch. In the desert, I will reduce these pressures by a third.

All this time, perhaps just over half an hour, the engine has been running, I screw the carburettor back to normal tickover, check the oil pressure (should be between 2 and 6 lbs./sq. inch), look around the campsite, light a cigarette and grin, and drive off.

I drive at a steady 40 mph on the straight flat roads, for about eight hours in the day, stopping to check the oil twice, fill up with petrol once, and urinate three times. Through the villages, when the locals wave and smile, all mornings I smile back, but rarely in the afternoons. My face is tight with fatigue when I stop. I have noticed, however, that the horn just refuses to work before noon, though today (26th November) it came on strong and managed a strangled bleep at 10.45 a.m.

Putting up camp, first, obviously, the kettle on for coffee or tea. Then the tent set, sleeping bag aired over the car's warm bonnet, a cup of coffee and a cigarette when I do *nothing*. My meal for the evening may be a sandwich, or sardines, or eggs, plus a vitamin pill and the third iron tablet of the day. My sister, Geraldine, a student midwife, procured them for me; the tablets are national health supplies to pregnant women.

After I have eaten, I have a few moments of utter wretchedness, a physical reaction to the day. In front of me is the paperwork. Normally, when I'm alone for days, I can write like fury, bits of a novel I may be working on, a plan, letters, notes, as many as 7,000 words in a day. But here, in the evenings, lying on the ground looking at the dark sky and waiting for the moon, it is an effort to keep up with letters to people who are interested, to friends, parents, even to Fiona, and the newspaper, which may pay for the ring. Sometimes I rationalise. I am very good at that. Last night, for example, I was asleep at 7.30, convinced I would write in the morning, yet knowing I wouldn't. I am too eager on the road each day. But I talk to myself, tell myself what's happening, where exactly I am, how I'm not really alone, and in the end, I can write. I have been doing it now for three hours.

Then, the quota done, a cigarette, beams at no one in particular, an ignorant look at the sky. I must learn how to recognise the stars one day, and soon. In about ten minutes, the typewriter packed away, the petrol can it is resting on and the water-can I am sitting on, packed away, the hurricane lamp hanging from a brolly which is stuck in the roof rack, packed away, all done, then I will get into the sleeping bag and sleep, as every night, the sleep of the just. I am involved to capacity; there is danger ahead, each passing moment will be important. I feel very fine about what's happening. And I sleep quickly. I have not done that since I was a child....

On November 26, I passed a police checkpoint, and asked about the Landrovers. They had not passed, and as I had seen neither the Cowboys nor the Scruffs, so I became the leader. I asked the policemen to tell the others I had passed them, and we chuckled happily at the incongruity of the situation. By evening, I had covered 222 miles, with the energy still to write to a number of people about what was happening.

I found Algerians more attractive than Moroccans. Shopping on my first day there, Alexa attracted her usual large crowd and barrage of questions, and people were eager to show me around the shops. Admittedly, they hit me for cigarettes in the end, but in Morocco, for that service, I would have had to give my soul to get away. The countryside was boring, through flat rounded hills and squat villages, trees where men worked pruning. I was in third gear perhaps six times in the whole day.

All the children laughed and pointed at the car, which was funny. There they were, riding scraggy donkeys, in rags, flogging bloody just-killed chickens to motorists with waves of their hands, and they found me funny. There was a strange mixture of ancient and modern, epitomised by an Arab in flowing burnoose, turban, a shotgun strapped across his back, riding a little phut-phut scooter with great dignity. Hundreds of people in each village were just sitting, looking at the road, and in crowds on the pavement, milling nowhere. I could see there was a great drive for education – many of the tots carried school bags – but it seemed that two generations had to waste and die because they did not know enough.

On November 27, at lunchtime on a beautiful clear day, I drove into Algiers. My first impression of the city was that it was rotting, pieces falling off and crumbling to dust, populated by people in an awful hurry to live and die before the city disappeared, all in the clear setting on a perfect blue bay. But everyone was friendly, and I was directed to the Central Post Office where I mailed off articles and letters, then had a salad lunch in a small restaurant on a hill, sitting in the window to keep an eye on the car. After further enquiries, I found the British Consulate, and went in to try and collect any available information on the Sahara crossing.

While in the waiting room, dressed in my usual driving

gear of jeans, cowboy boots, an old shirt, and goggles, and ignored by the receptionist, a door opened and the consul, a Mr. Harcombe, asked me if I owned the Austin 7 outside. I said I did, and followed him down to it. He asked me if I was going across the Sahara. I said I planned to, and he sighed with obvious exasperation. He walked around Alexa, quite beside himself, and, at a temporary loss for words, kicked her.

"Look at it!" he shrieked, "just look at it! Those tyres, for a start, they won't last a day. I have a friend who has just come up the desert trail – in a Landrover! – and his tyres were torn to *ribbons*. You haven't a chance, not a *chance!*"

Mr. Harcombe then went on at great length and with some relish, to describe other deficiencies in my car. At the end of his tirade I asked him for travel information, and we went to his office for a talk. He advised me, if I persisted in the ludicrous attempt to drive South, at least to join the Landrover convoy. The lead Landrover had arrived that morning. They were, he said – and at the time I believed him – a well-equipped outfit and might take me with them.

When I left, with no real information on desert conditions, I was extremely depressed. Would every official be like this? I decided there was nothing for me to find in the city and at 4 o'clock, began driving south. On the way out of Algiers, I met the main body of the Landrover convoy coming in. We honked horns at each other, stopped, and talked. They were as loaded with equipment as I had been told, and had heard I was chasing them. A good deal of ribaldry was directed at Alexa.

I camped with them that night at a small square overlooking the sea. Tim Bailey, the leader, told me he had originally planned to go through the Sudan, but the visas he had arranged to obtain for his charges had been withdrawn when it was learned, through publicity, that the convoy was bound for white South Africa. Most of the others came over and talked to me while waiting an hour and a half for an impressive kitchen to be erected, among them an American, Ray Saunders, and an Englishwoman, Ursula Carmen. I had coffee going quickly on my little stove, and was in the peculiar position of being host for an hour. I was tucked up in bed, having fed myself and given away 17 cups of coffee, before the first food was produced by the convoy's cooks for the day. One Landrover, I was told, was missing that night, out searching for information. The whole expedition was called Siafu Safari, after an East African ant that allows no obstacle to stop it. Someone said then that they would no doubt catch me in the desert, and there was short discussion of possible situations where I would need rescue.

Next day, Tim decided to move camp to an area of sand and dunes a couple of miles away, where his convoy could test their ability on sand. He said rather distantly that I could join them if I wished. Two Landrovers made it to the top of the dune with little trouble, two more bogged in the sand, and the fifth drove for five yards, hauling a trailer, and promptly broke a half-shaft. Alexa was able to get halfway up the dune, after numerous attempts, before sticking fast. Despite a lot of help, and sand-mats, I was never able to drive her to the top. Worried by the morale of the safari, which seemed to me to be riddled with backbiters and complainers, I said goodbye and drove off south again, through Algiers, toward the desert.

On November 28, there was a Kafkaesque incident which became an article for the *Irish Independent*. I arrived in Blida, a large town thirty miles south of Algiers, at 2.30 in the afternoon, sweating out an empty petrol tank. Due to a confusion of signs, I was directed up a narrow alley full of wailing music and people hawking vegetables. As usual, everyone stopped what they were doing and looked at the car. I asked the way to a bank, having about nine shillings (45p) in Algerian currency on me, and was told there was one in the main square. I ran out of petrol parking the car.

Immediately, small children surrounded us both. The banks were closed, said a shopkeeper, but certainly they would open at three o'clock. I waited, sitting on the car. The crowd grew; other cars took diversions until bodies were eight deep on to the road and under the arcades that surrounded the square. Occasionally, one or more children swung off the right headlamp, which is loose and needs to be tightened. I stood up and swore at them in a loud voice, making threatening gestures, and they backed off, but three minutes later they were doing it again. Men pushed through the crowd, cuffing the children, to ask for cigarettes. I kept repeating I wasn't American. They persisted, reeling off brand names hopefully. I kept smiling and said I was *un Anglais*, an Englishman.

But this was curious, one of these loafers spoke English, in a rusty inexperienced way, with an Irish brogue, and when I looked closer I saw he had blue eyes, which were very watery. I asked him who he was, and he chuckled, but when I asked him what he was doing there, he pushed back through the crowds and I never saw him again. He was wearing Arab dress, in contrast to the cheap cotton westernised clothes of most of the men. Could he have been a deserter from World War Two? I thought it likely.

Finally, three o'clock came, and the bank remained shut. Oh no, said another man, they all close at two o'clock for the day, and could I give him some American cigarettes? A pickle. Little money, no petrol, and the chance of the car being wrecked by urchins. Then a saviour arrived, in the shape of a very slick fellow in a blue mackintosh with a loud enough voice to drive the children away for five minutes at a time. But the crowd was still growing, men hanging around arcade pillars, nothing to do but look at the car and ask for cigarettes. Slicker, and a boy called Mahmoud, brought me to a shop. The shopkeeper listened to my tale with a serious face, phoned the bank, and the bank director came down. He vetted my $10 travellers' cheques, and gave me some money, all of us sitting around on flimsy wooden chairs looking casual, like those photos of small businessmen one sees in Mediterranean villages. It was a relief, when I walked back to the car, to find it still on four wheels.

Slicker brought me a can of petrol in return for twenty Spanish cigarettes, which he saved until nightfall, out of respect for the Muslim feast of Ramadan. I bought roughly two gallons at the standard rate, about 9/- a gallon, to get me out of town. Thinking I might pick up coupons in Medea, a town twenty miles away up in the Atlas Mountains, I drove there and camped for the night. But the bank in Medea had no tourist coupons for petrol (at 4/6 a gallon) so I had to drive back to Blida next day, and keep an appointment with Mahmoud, which my terrible urge to hurry had prompted me to break.

Mahmoud was in the square promptly at 9.30. He stood on the running board of the car and directed me to a friend of his who would guard Alexa for a shilling, and then we went into the bank. It was an imposing building, obviously built by the colonial French, with a policeman outside. Inside, there were cubicles, a man in each, writing and muttering. It was very quiet, and there were no customers. I asked for the exchange desk. A fat boy took my order for Algerian currency. Then the policeman came in and ordered Mahmoud outside. Fat boy asked for my passport, my currency slip stating how much money I had brought into Algeria, my vehicle registration certificate, and later, almost every bit of paper I had. Each time, he solemnly brought out a folder, put my piece of paper inside, and ran upstairs.

I spent the time walking in circles, looking at the floor, and occasionally at the men working. There was a loud buzz from time to time, and one of the men jumped up and rushed away. Five minutes later he was back, there was a silence, then another buzz, and another man jumped up and rushed away. Meanwhile, fat boy returned and asked for more paper, now my international driving licence, now the carnet-de-passage, now the chequebook. I continued to walk in circles, sometimes clockwise, once or twice anti-clockwise. Mahmoud stood outside in the rain under the stern eye of the policeman, and smiled when I looked out at him. Fat boy rushed up and down stairs, puffing inscrutably. All the men muttered and scratched with their pens. No customers came in, though once a postman delivered a brown package.

In this way, an hour passed.

Finally, fat boy came down, his face as blank as ever, and motioned me to the cash desk. The man there said "one hundred and fifty?" (litres, about 33 gallons) three times. Each time I solemnly nodded my head and said "yes". He shook his head, pursed his lips, and appeared to be waiting for something. It was not long in appearing. There was a perceptible change in the atmosphere when the Director swept down the stairs, his hand outstretched to shake mine, all my pieces of paper in his other hand. He asked about my health. I said it was fine. Then he said something quickly to the man behind the cash desk. The man hustled some papers around and rushed off. The Director smiled gently at me. I smiled back. The man returned, and gave yet more bits of paper to the Director.

The Director gave me back my own pieces of paper, stamped in all the correct places. He explained to me twice, in a reasonable manner, how much I was getting for my dollar cheques. The man behind the counter then curtly explained once, with written sums at which he pointed. I nodded whenever his pointing pencil stopped, stuffing pieces of paper into my wallet and pockets.

Everything, I gathered, was in order. I made a tentative step towards the door to check, and was allowed to go. The smile on the Director's face disappeared immediately I started to turn away. Mahmoud was outside, wet from the rain. I told him about the affair of buying some currency in his own country. He laughed. I felt good telling him about his own banking system. He did not mind the waiting, he said. After all, if he was not allowed in, I thought it would be something to learn how money works, even if it is a foreigner telling him. One day, perhaps, he will be old enough himself to enter a bank...

November 29, sitting cross-legged in my tent in a desert, high up in the Atlas Mountains, about 30 miles from Djelfa

The hurricane lamp is perched on the up-ended Primus stove box. I have eaten – scrambled eggs, bread and butter, pate and a tomato – plus a mug of coffee followed by tea and a vitamin pill.

Not long ago, in the general atmosphere of apprehension surrounding our camp together, one of the Cowboys had asked me if I was afraid of the trip ahead? I said I wasn't. I had been afraid, at nights, when I was at home planning the journey. But once it started there was too much to do, or I was too tired afterwards, to be afraid. Whenever I hit a bad road, I murmured, "you will see much worse than this", and it did not seem so bad. The car always ran smoothly. It was still running smoothly, but I had two shocks to knock me out of my ignorant confidence.

Both came yesterday, climbing those soft sand dunes. The first was how easy it is to bog down in the sand, and how difficult to dig Alexa out. The second was the extreme facility with which that Landrover broke its half-shaft.

In a way, the second bothers me more than the first. I have detailed information on the road, and later the track, and while there is certainly the prospect of great fields of sand, it should be beaten hard by now. The travelling season in the Sahara started on October 15th, six weeks ago. Anyway, I expected to dig my way across, or be towed, and have resigned myself to either eventuality. But a broken half-shaft is a different matter. That the Landrover was greatly over-loaded, as well as towing a trailer, has been commented on since I first heard about the convoy in Spain. Yet I will be loaded to capacity on one stage of the crossing, and when calculating spare parts to bring with me, I had to set a place to stop. Weight was one factor, money another.

I stopped buying spares before I bought a half-shaft.

Where does one stop? It might seem necessary to a worrier – as I appear to be just now – to tow along another complete Austin 7 for spares. I have enough with me to repair the brakes, change the springs, and strip the engine three times. There are two spare wheels, a puncture outfit, plus two jacks and a number of thick wooden boards to stand them on. I am carrying five gallons of oil, and twenty-five gallons of petrol, and food for two weeks at least. There is nothing for me to do but stop worrying about that Landrover. I must continue to speak to myself, saying I should drive carefully.

There are 32,856 miles on the clock. I have been on the road 17 days, and covered 2,636 miles, an average of 155 miles/day. As the whole journey is about 10,500 miles, that means I am about a quarter done, but it is the easiest quarter. There are five stages; London – Algiers, Algiers – Kano, Kano – CAR, the Congo, and then Uganda – South Africa. Of these, I am terrified about the second and fourth stages, and beginning the second stage right now. As to that question; yes, I am frightened, but strangely not nearly so much as I was in London. Perhaps my imagination has packed up for the duration, perhaps it is the fact that I am acting now, perhaps I want to see what will happen. Doing this, each moment becomes precious, demanding attention. I am aware of being alive.

Of course, reality was sitting in this tent with the moon outside so bright that men were working, a tractor near me by its headlamps, and behind me was a 32-year old car with all my supplies to remain travelling. I was relying on this car to get me through, and tried not to think too much about it. It seemed so fragile, a delicate civilised thing in a land that was becoming more and more brutal.

When I was walking after dinner, I thought about being alone, and how it was once so reassuring that there used to be a God. I argued this with the Landrover group. They thought He helped. I know He doesn't. I said it was cheating if you chose this situation, and then appealed to Him if you were in trouble. Trouble is coming, and I am deeply interested to see what I will do. It is easy to be an atheist day to day, but what will I do at the crunch? Will I blame anyone but myself? I hope not.

30 November, Guardaia, about 400 miles south of Algiers; day's mileage, 217

Guardaia is an oasis town out of the Arabian Nights, on the northern fringes of the Sahara Desert, though from Laghout the last 130 miles has seemed like desert to me. Tonight, at last bathed, and with clean clothes, I am staying in a hotel. It will be my last hotel for a month. Tomorrow, the road continues south to El-Golea. After that, there is 1,500 miles of desert track, over stone and sand, until Nigeria. It will be pretty bad. I will worry about it when I get there.

Last night I camped in the shelter of a small ledge on the fringe of the desert, but even there the wind was strong. Today it has been terrific, gusts up to 60 mph, with sand flowing in streams across the road. How vast this country is! I have driven across a huge plain, with knobbles of hills, worn round and striated by the wind, marching into the distance along the road. I have been awed by the prospect ahead. It seemed that Alexa would stop before I had driven five miles, but she has taken two hundred miles without a murmur.

Once, forgetting, I ran out of petrol in the shrieking gale. This meant pouring in another five gallons, with the unwieldy can and a small funnel. What a job! Petrol sprayed all over the road, the back of the car, my feet, anywhere but into the tank. I must beware of such situations.

Sitting in an old car, one feels each jar and shudder intimately. I find my emotions are directly tied to the car's behaviour. When the wind gusts, it is terrifying; the car digs in and loses five miles an hour. I lean forward, my shoulders tense, in some way urging the car forward. I have to tell myself to stop, that I am not doing any good, that Alexa is in fact a car and not a horse. But the horse syndrome is strong. I indulge in fantasy, sitting there with miles rolling under me, imagining a heart and lungs and muscles in this complicated piece of machinery I enter each day. And in the mornings, looking out of the tent with the kettle boiling, and a rope stretched from the tent-pole to one door handle, I see the car as a projection of the Great Earth Mother, supplier of all needs, comforter, transportation, bed. If ever she stopped and I was unable to fix her, my first impulse would be to howl.

Camels, like old headmasters, ponder with dignity and an odd outrage the car as it passes. They also remind me of Charles de Gaulle, especially a back view with the head turned in profile. There is sometimes a bundle by the side of the road. I pass, and look back and see it is a man curled up against the wind. What is he doing there? There are no sheep in sight, no camels, nothing but wind howling through telegraph wires, and flying sand. He is just there.

So far, except along the Moroccan coast, it has not been hot. With the wind coming from the west, I have had to wear my fur-lined jacket and scarf for most of the day. I had expected the nights to be cold, but in the daytime the Sahara should be hot. I am still 750 miles from the Tropic of Cancer. Perhaps after that, things will hot up a little

Algerians are very nice. A generality, but it is true for me. I have not met a bad one yet. There are all sorts of stories one hears about stealing in North Africa, and I take precautions, but I find people are sympathetic to Alexa. They shout at us, hoot their horns, crowd around perhaps dangerously when we stop, but they think Alexa beautiful (and I forgive anything after that), always asking to look at the engine. None of my outside baggage has been disturbed so far. Policemen go out of their way to be helpful. They salute smartly, are polite in asking questions, and have stopped traffic to let Alexa through. It may be that I get special treatment for a venerable car. Once, two motor-cycle policemen waved me down, just to look at Alexa, then gave me a front and back escort to where I was going. Mr Harcombe, the British Consul in Algiers, was sceptical when I told him about this. Poor, narrow man. He does not think much of Algeria. But the French have gone, and so far as I can see Algeria is becoming itself, with joy at the prospect.

Outside, as always, it is a clear black sky, with a luminous moon approaching full. My clothes are stewing in the sink. Down the corridor the radio wails, familiar to radio hams on short wave tuning through the channels. But the sound is not from a faraway country tonight, it is right here.

I have to grease the car tomorrow, and I worry at my impatience. Sometimes I get momentum packing in luggage, and just carry out the usual basic tests before driving off, instead of taking pains to check less obvious faults. It is

3,000 miles since the last full grease job. I cannot afford to take risks. The differential also needs oil, another job which is easy to put off, until disaster.

Having no one to talk to who speaks my own language, it is often useful to write down what has to be done, as I just have, so I can see it printed in front of me. It is almost like someone replying. l bet that other people who were alone found this was true also. I can think of tasks, especially when driving, but when I have the time to do them, somehow I forget. A bad habit.

Skins of civilisation are peeling off me. I find myself more and more brusque towards people who might endanger the car, more able to take quick decisions. I think that the future, rough as it will be, will bring an increase in this peeling. A good thing too; three years in London is time to collect a lot of rubbish.

On December 1 I serviced the car and talked to a young English couple – Rupert Oliver and his wife – in a Landrover. I asked them to post my articles and letters back home, as I could not wait, and it was a Sunday. I discovered a slow puncture in one tyre, and changed the wheel. I left Guardaia in mid-afternoon. Fifteen miles later, there was a smell of petrol, and I found a leak on the pipe to the carburetter. Some Germans coming north from In Salah stopped to talk, and thought I was a little daft, but they said if I took care I would make it. I heard later that they told everyone else that I was going to kill myself, which made me pretty angry. Why couldn't they have said that to my face? Surely they knew the desert is like a small knitting circle, and all gossip is repeated for everyone to hear?

On December 2 at El Golea I faced a hard choice. There were no facilities for changing money. The nearest place was Guardaia, 163 miles behind me. It was possible I might change money at an airport, either at El-Golea, or 254 miles up the track at In Salah. When I checked the airport in town, I found no aircraft were expected, so facilities were closed, but perhaps there would be one tomorrow? In the spare petrol cans I had ten gallons of petrol, the capacity to carry ten more gallons, and the car's tank was full. I had coupons for another five gallons. Thirty-five miles outside El Golea the road stops and the track starts. It goes through In Salah, and Tamanrasset is another 434 miles on from there, nearly 5,000 feet up in the mountains. I had seven dinars in coin, about 14 shillings (70p).

That was the choice in front of me. Enough petrol to make Tamanrasset on normal roads, but the tracks are distinctly abnormal. In theory, I cannot change money for the next 688 miles. Should I drive back to Guardaia to wait for the banks to open, using 8 gallons of petrol on the round trip, and declare two and a half days wasted? Or do I drive on and check out the airport at In Salah, knowing it is the jumping-off point for many of my companions going into the desert?

I chose to go on.

I was facing a stretch of road through to In Salah which the AA guide had some reservations about… "Improvements are being made to this sector, which is at present very rough going. Keep tyre pressure low and do not exceed 30 mph in the heat of the sun. This is the most dangerous part of the route as far as tyres are concerned. There are iron or stone beacons every 5 kilometres."

There were 33,343 miles on the clock; 3,123 miles since leaving home 19 days ago. I entered the desert proper on the track, called *La Piste*, at 1.45pm that day, with 33,289 miles on the clock. It has been difficult since. I was shocked at the hammering taken by Alexa. Used to bowling along at 40 mph on the flat, I naturally tried to push too fast. The shaking slowed me down, and I experimented. It seemed my best speed was 15 mph, and those 1,500 miles of track to Nigeria looked an awfully long way. It was not pessimistic to say I might make Kano, and tarmac again, by Christmas.

As the sun went down and an absolute stillness fell over the land, I managed to pause long enough to appreciate where I was. With a full moon I could work greasing the car and doing small jobs. Pottering around, humming snatches of music-hall songs I had not heard in years, it struck me that I should be lonely. But I wasn't. There was no one to see for miles around, just incredibly vast stretches of land, wasted and barren. I felt content, without needing someone else. I wondered if this feeling would last? I admitted that my imagination had gone to sleep, to my relief, but sometimes it woke up and prodded me. A moth flew around the hurricane lamp. Behind me, the moon was so bright one could see all the dips and shadows of surrounding country. Apollo Ten would be heading for the moon in a few days, and I was here.

I wonder how many moths have died, attracted by the shining moon?

There had been some small troubles with the car. It was difficult to start this morning, taking five minutes. At noon, in El Golea, the starter mechanism fused and seized. I by-passed the wiring, and used the fixed handle to start the engine. This evening, using the Primus stove as a blow-torch, I loosened up the starter arm. I have been thinking since about this. A screwdriver stretched between the negative lead (Austin 7's have a positive earth) and the starter confirmed that the motor itself is undamaged. It was only the small connection arm. I believe I can rig a cardboard and insulation-tape device which will stop the connection arm shorting out, as long as I am careful pouring oil into the engine, for it was oil that caused the trouble in the first place. The filler cap is located just over the starter motor, and with gallon cans I often spill oil over parts of the engine. I shall have to give myself yet another warning. It is undignified getting out to wind Alexa up in front of half a hundred staring little Arab boys.

Both tyres are getting bald, but are standing the strain well. I was told bald tyres are best for the desert. Sand seems to have disappeared, and now it is hard-baked clay under me, with small eddies of dust.

Fort Mirabel, once manned by the Foreign Legion, was three miles behind, now a lonely and deserted building. It appeared suddenly inside a huge hole in the land, which usually means water is present. Four French people in an English-registered Landrover were washing themselves by the side of a well. I had passed them, and been passed in turn, three times. They were somewhat surly. I believed they were pretty upset because, no matter how fast they drive, they could not lose me. They drove far too fast. First they shook their roof-rack off, I passed them, they rushed past an hour later. Then their electrical cut-out went, I passed them and again they galloped by me. After the waterhole, when Alexa pottered down the hill and up the other side, I could see how quickly they dried themselves and soon they were past me once more. We should meet again, the tortoise and the hare.

December 3, covered 120 miles, now 50 miles from In Salah

To imagine the condition of the track, one has to visualise the back of a giant hand, with the skin torn off, so bones are visible, and lay those hands down edge to edge for hundreds of miles. Add 1-in-5 gradients, boulders, scattered rocks, sand in 25-yard stretches, water every 100 miles if you can find the well, a sun that is getting hotter and hotter, and perhaps three other people in sight per day. Imagine that and you have an idea of the Hoggar piste across the eastern Sahara Desert.

And there is more than one trail. There are markers every 500 metres for the official trail, so you can see which direction to drive. But tyre marks stretch off to better pieces of ground, with fewer pot-holes. Twice, today, I followed these other tracks. Each time I kept a wary eye on the markers. When I was level with one I would be anxiously scanning for the next. It was dangerous. Unofficial trails were made by lorries which know the route. Gradually the markers got further and further away. You see tracks of lorries which chickened-out, and headed back towards the markers, but always there is an unofficial track marching blithely over an unknown hill. I was tempted to take it, cut short a few hundred yards maybe, stay on better ground. After all, the tracks must lead to In Salah, so what is the danger? Yet if I lost a marker and panicked, that would be it. I know I should turn east and keep driving and there would be the trail again. But could I be sure?

From In Salah, I expected to be forced to drive in convoy, so there would not be any danger, but I was tempted today. Nine hours in the driving seat over roads which buck and shudder can induce a peculiar state of mind, where useless risks are inviting.

This morning I learned a lesson about myself. It wasn't a nice one. When I tried to start the car on the handle, as the starter still did not work, nothing happened. I was up at dawn, hoping to make In Salah by dusk. But when I cranked and cranked, the engine would not start. First I checked the electrics. Because of my ignorance, I thought that if there was no spark in the distributor, then the condenser had gone. I have one spare, and changed them over. Then I checked the battery leads, which were OK. Two cigarettes smoked rapidly, and a truck ground past. I waved casually. There was no minus reading on the ammeter when I turned the ignition on. Any attempt at hot-wiring the car produced smoke from the distributor, and I hastily uncoupled the wire and pondered frantically. Perhaps the carb? No, that was clean. From the recesses of my memory came the right way to check the spark, flicking the points while holding the rotor arm in an active position on the distributor cap. I tried that...a spark! It must be the carburetion. What about a faulty ignition switch, though? Turn the key again, a reading for two seconds, then no reading. Ah, perhaps that wire that by-passed the starter? Yes, it was loose, a bad job. I used my vocabulary on myself, with some enthusiasm. But when I cranked there was still a dead engine. Carefully, I looked at the carburettor, and absent-mindedly primed the petrol pump. *No petrol.* Fool! Of course, I have no petrol gauge, but I can usually tell I am short because of the mileage. All that fuss and worry had been for nothing. I had filled half an hour with panic-stricken fears. This will not do at all. I must trust the previous three month's work to know that, basically, the car is sound. For the whole morning I scowled at everything.

At noon I met a Scottish motor-cyclist who had come up from Agadez, 1,000 miles away. He looked very burnt by the sun, but he had made it. Naturally, we stopped to gossip. He said, "that's the first time I've seen one of those here," and I laughed. But a truck with his luggage and perhaps ten Arabs hanging on for dear life was rattling out of our sight, so we could not talk for long. I told him to watch out for a convoy of six Landrovers. He told me to watch out for three girls, two Americans and a Welsh girl called Jackie, that he had last seen in Tamanrasset. They were hitch-hikers, he said.

December 4, In Salah

This morning I drove into In Salah. For months, I had imagined my meeting with the Commandant here. Now that Algeria is independent, the Commandant has been replaced by a sub-prefect. Motorists who wish to drive across the Sahara must report to the sub-prefect, who was supposed to examine vehicles to determine whether or not they were fit for the journey. Quite obviously, I was worried how he would react to Alexa.

I had pictured arguments with him, over and over again. He was supposed to be a gruff old Frenchman, ex-military, with a certain elan. Emphasising such daring as there was in my own journey, I expected to move him finally from his absolute refusal to allow me to continue, to a position where he relented and appointed another traveller in a strong vehicle to look after me.

In reality, the sub-prefect was a young, French-educated Algerian with heavy glasses, who did not even bother to look at the car. He will telegraph ahead to Tamanrasset, at no charge to me, to tell them I am coming, and should arrive in an estimated four days, on December 9. He also said it was not necessary to travel in convoy, although advisable. The track was clear, better than from El Golea, and I should avoid sandy patches.

Ah, I had learned my lesson there. I ran into one patch this morning at about 9.30, and bogged down, the first time on

route. Muttering to myself, and eyeing the clear track five
yards to my right, I dug the car out. That should have been
it, but no, a stubborn streak asserted itself, and I approached
the very next stretch of sand at speed. The car bogged down
again. My language became lurid, directed at myself, and I
dug the car out a second time. There was no more trouble
until I reached town. Surely I will be all right here, I
thought? Almost immediately, the car went in again, and
within seconds was being swarmed over by Arab boys,
chattering nineteen to the dozen. I was so angry I refused an
offer from the police to pull me out, and dug furiously until
the car was free.

More news of the road society. The four Scruffs I had met
at the bottom of Spain left In Salah this morning, a few
hours before I arrived. Everyone was amused by them,
flashing around in their yellow van, with numerous
conferences on what to do next. I was astonished they were
ahead of me. They must have taken the route directly south
of Oran, and cut across east to In Salah. Perhaps I would
meet them in Tamanrasset?

Aside from the Sub-Prefect, I met another Algerian. He
had a small beard, spoke English, and was the Director of
Education for 3,500 square miles of the surrounding desert.
The problem I had with money, needing change for dollar
cheques, he solved for me. On top of that, he invited me to
dinner. During Ramadan, no one eats, drinks, smokes or
fornicates from sunrise to sunset. When night comes there is
a positive orgy. It was marvellous to speculate away the
afternoon on what I would eat for dinner. I filled all the
petrol cans and my water-tank, fixed the starter motor with
cardboard and insulating tape, and washed myself
thoroughly from a tap by the petrol station. At 5 o'clock,
dressed as best I could, I drove to see Mr Mohammed Touati,
the director (there are many directors in Algeria).

What a tremendous night it was! We ate, soup, chicken
that fell off the bone, peppers in sauce, rice, fresh crisp bread,
salad, tomatoes, followed by coffee. Gradually, our hunger
diminished, and we began to talk, about England, Israel,

religions, gambling, all things relating to each other. I was almost drunk with pleasure. In a stark white room, punctuated by children's wailing and laughter, with books in all languages scattered over packing cases, the table and three chairs, the room's only furniture, how we talked! He told me about the Pan-African Movement, we argued about capitalism, differed, smiled, and wandered on. His books included those by Che Guevara, Nkrumah, du Bois. His family was a rich one, and he could be a capitalist if he chose to, he admitted. But he felt that almost every contact he had with other people was hypocritical.

Afterwards he piled the table with food, sardines, cheese, coffee, chocolate, enough for days. It was almost too much to take away, but he insisted. I returned the hospitality with English cigarettes and tea, a poor exchange but all I could spare.

Tonight I am sleeping in a private room next to the student dormitory, after playing three games of chess, one to a draw, the other two lost. The teachers were from all over the Arab world. For the first time I have been privy to local opinion. One hears a lot about the kibbutz in Israel, but nothing about these in Arab countries. Are there kibbutzim in Algeria? To think I was on a week's standby as a pilot to fight for Israel in the Six Day War in June of last year! Madness.

Ahead of me now, the AA guide became even more cautious, claiming only a road in "fair condition", with construction taking place (that had all stopped with Algeria's independence). With 435 miles between In Salah and Tamanrasset, all there was in between was desert and a few lonely wells, if I could find them.

December 5, 102 miles south of In Salah, averaging 26 miles per gallon. Camped alone on the side of the road

When one visualises the Sahara, one thinks of sand, but up to now, with the exception of swirls blown across the road, the terrain has been a dry reddish clay. Each day has been comfortable, like an Indian summer at home, and there have been no real difficulties. Last night I was enthusiastic about my luck, that it was running well. It still is, for I have covered my planned hundred miles in a day, but only just. The sand has appeared.

Yesterday I either dug myself out, or was pushed out, of three drifts. Each time it was my own fault, I was ignorant of conditions here. Where sand has collected on the track, other travellers have made detours over firmer ground. I have ploughed straight in and learned a few lessons.

Today I had no choice but to enter the drifts. There were no alternative routes. On the first two occasions, I patiently dug myself out, humming cheerfully, accepting it. The third time, with a drift twenty-five yards long, and very deep, I thought I would try caution. Leaving the car in front of the drift, I spent a quarter of an hour digging, before concluding it would take a week. Either I run at it, and then dig the car out, or I detour, and I chose to detour. We sank fast within ten yards, and stuck there. That was that. I removed the load of petrol, 20 gallons, plus 4 gallons of oil, shoved the sand-mats under the rear wheels, and dug. No amount of engine gunning would move the car, so I sat down with Albert Camus' *The Rebel* and waited for help.

After half an hour, a military six-wheeled truck of Russian manufacture came by, out of In Salah, and within ten minutes Alexa was on the other side of the drift. The truck left me while I piled the petrol into the back seat, and a quarter of an hour later, I was stuck again. This time the track was badly marked, and I was off it again.

By mid-day, having set off from In Salah at 8 o'clock in the morning, I had covered 20 miles. The 400 miles to Tamanrasset looked impossible. I was furious, storming away in the driving seat after the fifth drift, waiting, just daring another sand-drift to stop me. What I would have done I cannot say. I felt I was being picked on, which was absurd. There were sand drifts in the afternoon. I hurled Alexa at each of them, engine gunning in third gear, myself tensed and hunched over the steering wheel. Each time we were successful in staggering through. By 5 o'clock the day's hundred miles had been done. I looked for a suitable place to camp, found one, drove the car off the track and promptly stuck again. This time it was fine, the day was over and I laughed.

I ate well tonight, but my manners are deteriorating. Without another person around, if I am really hungry, I can eat in an unashamedly ravenous manner. There were sardines mashed up with cheese, bread broken and stuffed in pieces into my mouth between noisy cups of coffee. In my attempt to preserve order on this drive, I must stop this behaviour. I should try to make a ceremony out of eating, for no other reason than being human and being English. Eating like an animal will lead to not shaving, or cleaning my teeth, to forgetting or not bothering to clean the air-filter, or check the tyres, or to fill the engine with oil. This trip will end because of something stupid, and I cannot afford to let myself slip. In fact I must be more keen on small ceremonies than I normally am, for normally I have no time for them.

If I run into no more banks of sand, I should make Tamanrasset by the day after tomorrow. But it is too much to hope for that. Still, we are over 2,000 feet up now, and Tamanrasset is at 4,800 feet. There cannot be a great deal of sand until the next stage, the worst, from Tamanrasset to Agadez.

(Next day was December 6th 1968. I hit a sandbank at noon, was pushed out by six friendly Frenchmen, and that evening I stupidly ate more sardines from an open tin. All night I was sick with ptomaine poisoning, and at 12.15 am on December 7th, groggy from the effects, I drove into a steel barrier by the fort at In Ekker...)

CHAPTER 7
The Sahara

After the crashing stopped, I switched off the ignition, for the engine was no longer running. I opened the door and stepped out. The front of the car was crumpled, there were deep gouges under the windscreen, and the bonnet lay 15 yards away, almost torn in two. If I had been driving a modern saloon car, I thought, I would have been decapitated. A man was walking quickly from the fortress towards me. I started swearing, at the barrier, at him and at myself. For the first time, perhaps after long practice at the roads, I was fluent, mixing English and French in a long bitter stream.

But in the car's engine, everything seemed in place. The radiator was bent like a sprung bow, although no water was leaking from it. I started the engine, dubiously, and it burst into life. "It works", I said in English, to no one in particular, and I turned it off. The man, a soldier, reached me and addressed me in furious Arabic. I told him shortly to speak French. More men arrived, one of them reading a comic book about a French pilot who flew with the RAF in the last war. A goat came strutting across looking for something to eat. We all looked at Alexa.

I tried to straighten out the bonnet with my hands, without success. I was thirsty, and asked for water. A man gave me a bottle. Then they all looked at the steel barrier. A corporal tried to lift it back on to its stand. It was bent and too heavy for six men. I felt suddenly pleased that I had broken something belonging to people who had put this incredibly stupid thing here in the first place. After a few minutes it dawned on me that my windscreen and headlights were unbroken, and that except for the bent radiator and the smashed bonnet, there seemed to be little wrong with Alexa.

I asked to see the chief of the camp. The corporal, who appeared to be in charge of the post, said the chief was 20 miles away, at the other end of the tarmac road. I said I would drive there, and he said it was not allowed. What would happen then? I asked. He said we must wait for the chief to arrive. How would the chief know he was required to arrive? He shrugged. Was there a telephone at the place? There wasn't. The corporal said that if a truck came by, going south, he would be able to get a lift and bring the chief back. Was a truck expected? He shrugged his shoulders again, looking at Alexa. Then he said, if my car went, we could both go and fetch the chief. I said there wasn't room for more than one person, and he grunted and turned away, and went off to look at the barrier. I walked over and sat again in Alexa. I was not feeling sick any more, just awfully detached and uncaring. I would not allow myself to believe that the trip was finished.

After an hour and a half of sullen misunderstandings, I ungraciously repacked some of my luggage and gave the corporal a ride in a bonnet-less Alexa to the main army camp at In Amguel to see his chief and to report the incident. For an hour I waited in the sun while the corporal talked leisurely to his friends, before he sauntered off to find the chief. I removed the headlights because the wings had been flapping dangerously in the wind, and lit cigarette after cigarette, ignoring the grins of the corporal's friends.

Finally a small man appeared with a star on each shoulder, and invited me to dinner. He said his mechanics would fix everything, which was an enormous relief. I learned later that he was extremely angry at the corporal of the small post because no man was at the barrier when I arrived. From my point of view, a barrier stuck across the road in the middle of nowhere, when drivers were still watching for ruts ten yards in front of their cars, should be manned every minute of the day. I felt it was absurd anyway, that there should be a barrier, but then I had hit it, and was biased.

December 7/8, static at In Amguel

At the army camp, the mechanics fixed the bonnet, re-wired the car (a bonus I felt was due), fixed the front lamps back on again, tightened down the wings, and generally made the car road-worthy. In between times, I was curious about the camp.

Apparently, when the French had Algeria, it was a top-secret establishment, and some form of atomic device was tested nearby. Now there was (said to be) little radio-activity, the French had left, and there remained only a shell, protected fiercely by a small Algerian garrison, but giving the impression of strength, when in reality, there was nothing at all. The army guards were all single men, and served one year each at the base. They were very kind, feeding me, giving me a bed, asking questions about the car, sharing without hesitation, not as rich men giving hand-outs, but as equals.

However, the conditions in which they lived were dreadful. The camp was wired for electricity, and piped for water. There were toilets and showers, all the civilised paraphernalia of a modern army. I worked in a garage full of French and Russian trucks, plus some British Landrovers. But though there was a noisy machine for generating electricity (right outside my room, it kept me awake until midnight), I could see hundreds of bulbs were missing and were not replaced. And the toilets did not flush, nor did water run from the taps and showers. Trucks were cannibalised to make other trucks work, and when I opened my small tool kit with fourteen spanners, the mechanics fell on it like hungry men. Inside their barriers of barbed wire, it was sad to see how truly ill-equipped they were. They were extremely generous with what they had.

December 9, In Salah to Tamanrasset

By noon, everything was fixed, ready to go. I knew the first hundred miles would show any damage to the engine. Tamanrasset was 114 miles away. The drive there, through the afternoon and early night, was a trial, more so because of two days rest from driving. I made it, asked about Siafu Safari, which should have overtaken me by now, and was told they were a mile out of town. I drove in complete darkness, looking for lights until I hit a patch of soft sand leading nowhere. For ten minutes I wallowed there, frightened, angry, utterly alone, before I managed to struggle out. On the way back into town I met two of the Scruffs, and four young English boys in a Landrover. They directed me to water, I filled my tank, and then drove to their camp. Safety.

There are only three Scruffs left; Bob, Stewart and Mick, I have learned their names. Jeff, who appeared the toughest when I met them in Spain, left Tamanrasset two days ago, saying he wanted to go back to England, and taking the carnet de passage with him by mistake. The Scruffs (though we are all Scruffs now in the middle of the desert), had telegraphed the police at In Salah to stop him, and they were stuck here, waiting, speaking no French, unable to leave without a carnet.

Bob, a wild man with ten feet of cloth wrapped around his head in Arab style, told me how ten of them had had the idea in England, to drive through Africa. As they stuck into it, buying a van and spares, a tent, supplies, people dropped out, until five of them set off. After the argument in Spain, four went on, but Jeff had been having doubts since In Salah. Second and third gear had gone on the van, and they had driven in first and fourth only. If they could get through the police post only half a mile away, they planned to go on to Nigeria. An American hitching north had lured Jeff away. Morale fluctuated, up one minute, down the next.

The four young boys were Tom – the leader – his brother
Bill, and two friends, Nigel and Chris. I don't think their
average age was more than 19. They had heard about me a
week ago, and had been trying to catch me ever since. They
must have passed In Amguel a few hours before I left the
camp, as they arrived at midnight tonight. Tom said he had
seen Siafu Safari a long way down the trail, and there
appeared to have been some sort of mutiny.

The boys are going through to Agadez, leaving tomorrow.
Their final destination is South Africa, but because they were
afraid of the Congo, they planned to ship their car from
Brazzaville to Luanda, Angola, and drive through from
there. I said there was a guerrilla war in Angola, but they did
not think it was serious, and anyway, it was better than the
Congo. I asked them if they would escort me to Agadez, and
warned them that Alexa cannot go very fast, and was prone
to sink in sand. I did not know how reliable the engine was
after the crash, which had spoiled her pretty looks. Tom said
it would be a pleasure to take me, and they would certainly
look after me. The others agreed.

Two French boys, one called Claude, had dinner with us.
They were hitching through to Central Africa. Claude had
tooth-ache; one side of his face is blown out like a balloon.
They will go through with the Scruffs if the police allow it.

Heading south from Tamanrasset, 261 miles to a desert
fort called In Guezzam, on the border between Algeria and
Niger, I faced what the AA guide thought was the worst part
of the journey. It warned that the route was not well-
defined, and there were no facilities at all on the way. It
advised travellers to follow, but not to get into, a set of lorry
tracks, which touched a line of cairns at intervals. "Avoid the
worst patches of soft sand, and do not lose sight of the
beacons". The guide warned that the route was constantly
changing because of sand-storms, and one should be
particularly careful about following tracks off the main
route. Immediately south of Tamanrasset there were fields
of broken stone, and descending the Hoggar Massif the
track passed though a rocky wilderness of jagged peaks,

rounded domes and flat-topped mountains. "This route is probably the most difficult part of the desert crossing." The track followed a series of dry river beds, 10 to 20 miles in length, bordered by rocky hills which eventually converged, forcing motorists to leave one valley for another. The only reliable local source of water was Tedjerine Well, just 37 miles south of Tamanrasset; "do not rely on water from desert wells, as it is often very limited and sometimes non-existent". The guide recommended reconnoitring on foot, and rushing any soft stretches. Sand mats and shovels must be carried, and it was important to watch out for transverse channels that led the motorist off the main track. Altogether, a daunting prospect.

December 10, camped in the desert

I spent the morning clearing Alexa with customs, with no trouble. Then I reported to the sub-Prefect to argue the Scruffs' case. Every argument I put forward was met with a further demand to look at my papers, but I managed to secure a promise that the Scruffs could continue next day (it was just a ruse to get me out of the way). The carnet was useless anyway, without Jeff, as it was made out in his name.

I left Tamanrasset at 12.30 with the four boys, and made 90 miles in the afternoon. Alexa stuck in the sand four times. Each time the others leapt out cheerfully and heaved me out in a couple of minutes. The trail was pretty good. They are all in bed now, and I am typing by the light of my hurricane lamp. I have just had tea with two extraordinary young French students, who are bedding down a few yards away.

About half an hour ago I became aware of an engine labouring, changing gear. After a minute I saw a glow over a hill to the south, and then a pair of yellow lights popped up and wavered towards me. I walked on to the track and waved them down. It was a Citroen 2CV. Inside, looking absolutely shattered, were the two students.

Night driving in the Sahara is dangerous, but supposed to be especially so between Tam and Agadez, as the track is badly marked for miles. I could not understand what they were doing on the road at 8 o'clock in the evening. They pointed to a rope drawn tight between the roof of the car and the chassis, and said the latter had broken in Agadez. They had to be back in Limoges, in central France, where they must register for a new university term. They had no money to get the chassis repaired, so they roped it to the car body and were going to drive all the way back! I hurried to make tea, and persuaded them to stop and sleep, as they had been driving continuously for the whole day. Those Citroens appear able to take desert conditions very well. Air-cooled engines, a high suspension and front wheel drive, particularly, were suitable for sand.

December 11

An extremely difficult day. Now camped by a well at In Guezzam, having had our passports stamped out of Algeria, and we should make Niger tomorrow. Though we made 150 miles, the trail had turned into huge plains of soft sand, stretching for miles and rimmed by irregular mountains. Twice, Alexa had to be towed, once for two miles. She sank innumerable times.

Everyone appeared cheerful tonight, as they were last night, but there is a brittle atmosphere, and tempers are shorter. Nigel, one of the boys, is most on edge, though he acts the friendliest. Bill is dour, Tom is constantly aware of his responsibilities, and Chris is quiet. They are really on holiday, and are sensibly equipped to handle most situations. I was rather lucky they were helping me, but they have become inclined to emphasise this.

 **CHAPTER 8**
Niger

Niger – Landlocked country of 489,000 square miles, capital Niamey, came under French rule in the late 1890's, and became independent in 1960. Surrounded by seven other countries, and one of the poorest in the world. Official language was French, and its major religions were either Islam or indigenous beliefs. The French had built passable roads to provide a land link with other central African colonies like Chad and the Central African Republic, and maintained real control of the country because the CFA, its currency unit, was directly linked to the French franc.

The AA guide was cautious about travel on its main north-south route via In Guezzam, Agadez and Zinder, no part of which was tarmac. The trail was marked by bidons, empty oil barrels, placed every 500 metres.

(December 12th to December 20th), 34,261 - 34,930 (669 miles) 4,041 - 4,710 miles from London

December 12th

I drove 86 miles today. We left In Guezzam being stared at by dozens of Arabs seated between the battlements of the *Beau Geste* fort at In Guezzam, who chattered amongst themselves. Our route took us over great beds of sand. We crossed into Niger at 7 am. Nigel and Chris had stomach upsets, and were no longer cheerful pushing Alexa out of the sand, into which she fell so many, many times. The last straw for them came at 4.30 this afternoon. They started to tow me through a heap of soft sand a quarter of a mile back. Then they stopped. Tom got out and said the clutch had gone.

I felt embarrassed. Nigel waved his arms and got a bit hysterical. I suggested we unload my car, I would take one of them with me, and we would drive to Agadez for a new clutch. Nigel walked around Alexa and began to berate me for taking her into the desert in the first place. They decided, next time I was stuck, they would leave me. Someone else coming along behind could help.

Five minutes after they had pushed me out, Alexa was in again. I watched them drive off with the setting sun behind them, but I did not say anything, nor cry out. Arabs appeared from nowhere, about 40 of them, probably Touregs. I hauled out my nylon rope, and organised them to pull the car out, which they did and then clamoured around for cigarettes. I gave out 20, 3 to the chief, and thinking I could catch the boys before nightfall, drove off quickly.

Alexa is now up to her chassis in a deep sand bed a quarter of a mile from where she last struck. I felt so bad. She will not move. All the Arabs who did not get cigarettes have been sitting in a circle looking at me. I have no more to spare and they won't help.

An hour ago I lay on my back with a cup of coffee beside me and looked at the sky. I was frightened. Now I am truly alone. I smoked four cigarettes, drank four coffees. What shall I do? Can I wait? No. Who is going to come through in the next few days? Would they help anyway? I would rather go on alone. Two Arabs, one young, one the old chief, squat by the coffee pot and stare at me typing. Twenty yards away through the soft sand, the ground is hard. Perhaps they will help me get Alexa there? How? And what about the next sand drift?

It is difficult to think coherently.

December 13th

Last night the two Arabs, with much sweat spent in 3 hours work, helped me out of the bed of sand. I gave them a pound of sugar and a cigarette each. They stole my rope and my favourite blue nylon shirt. Later, to calm myself, I began to read Albert Camus' *L'Etranger* again, with the young Arab looking over my shoulder. He pointed at various objects in the car, then at himself, nodded and smiled, and I said no. He made incomprehensible noises over my book, as if he was reading it. Twice he motioned that I should leave my car and sleep at the camp. Once he suggested he should get into my sleeping bag. Without being rude, I drove him off. I did not want my throat cut in the night, and he had already pulled a knife on me for bellowing at him when he tried to drink some of my coffee. I ignored the knife and carried on bellowing in English. When he had gone I tried to sleep, but something scuttled over my sleeping bag, and I thought it wiser to lock myself in the cramped car for the rest of the night.

This morning, after breakfast, three boiled eggs, bread and honey, porridge and coffee, I packed the car ready to go. My stomach was very tight. I kept speaking aloud, to hear my voice. "This could be the best day or the worst". I was afraid to be stuck in the sand. Unlike the earlier part of the desert, there was no fixed trail until about 150 miles from Agadez, and I was about 220 miles away. If I stuck in the sand, that was it. There was little chance of digging and pushing on to a hard trail; it was all soft. While the car moved it was possible to negotiate the sand. When it stopped, we sank. I told myself not to panic, resolved to take great care, and set off.

For three hours there were patches of soft sand. I could see by the colour of the ground when they were coming. Each time, I stopped and got out before the patch, looked around and tested the ground for the best route, backed up Alexa and charged at it. The trick was to change down gears very fast, from fourth to first, gunning the engine and slipping the clutch to keep momentum.

The strain of the trail told on the bent-bow radiator, and it sprang a leak at its base. I kept pouring water in until I ran out, and then I urinated into it, a desperate measure. By chance I spotted some goats, and stopped. Where there are animals there must be a well, I reasoned, and there was. A young Toureg with ten young girls and a large herd of animals were camped there. They acted as if they owned it, and before lowering the leather bucket for water, wanted something from me. I haggled in a detached manner, as if it was not important, and secured five gallons for two aspirins and two cigarettes. Three girls wanted cigarettes as well, and kept hacking and spitting great gobs into the deep well. They were very sullen when I wouldn't give them any. I stopped the leak with a rubber patch from my puncture outfit.

It is difficult to organise my thoughts, even about today, but soon afterwards I spied some sand-dunes and the trail markers disappeared. I stopped and wondered how I was to get through. Just then three tiny piccaninnies came running over the sand, waving at me. One was naked and black, the other two had little shirts on, and were Arab. They must have been four or five years old. They were very thin. I looked at them. They waved towards the dunes and nodded. Why not? Maybe they knew the way. I didn't.

They stood on my running boards and chattered, pointing in one direction, so I drove that way. Soon we were within the dunes, and they chattered and pointed another way. I followed directions, the car wallowing along in first and second gear, sometimes pointing right at a dune, then turning at the last moment to point at a second dune. I trusted them completely, wallowing between more dunes until, incredibly, we were through. In the distance, over on the right, I could see a trail marker pole. I roared away laughing, perhaps hysterically, for some time, then gave the children a piece of glucose each. They stared wistfully at my stale bread, so I gave them nearly all I had, and they ran off chattering.

With incredible luck I had managed by mid-day to cover 50 miles, and was growing confident. Then there was that familiar lurch, and the car stuck, Getting out was difficult, because I was shaking violently.

Ah well, I said, it's no good, you have no choice. Out came the improvised sand mats, and the shovel, and after three quarters of an hour I managed to get Alexa on to a rare piece of hard sand. Two Nigerien Landrovers went shooting by, going north. The first did not stop, which dismayed me, but the second did. After demanding to know why I was alone, the three men helped me over the final few yards of sand. The back window fell out. One of Alexa's headlamps has lost its glass.

In the afternoon, sandy patches became less frequent. I stuck once, digging myself out stoically, watched by an old Arab on a camel who made no move to help me, but still hit me for a cigarette afterwards. I told him to bugger off. A Swedish-German-French safari came up on me later, as I was filling the petrol tank. One of the men on it spoke excellent English, and we exchanged trail gossip for a while. He told me what had happened to the Scruffs, which made me both sad and angry.

Apparently, the Scruffs decided they would continue without their van, as it was in poor condition, and the border police at Tamanrasset had said that was fine. They had a large stock of petrol, which they gave to the Swedish-German-French safari in return for a lift to Nigeria. Leaving sugar in their van's petrol tank, and wrecking it in various ways to comply with customs regulations and avoid import duty, the Scruffs happily set off in the safari's two Landrovers and a jeep towards Niger.

At In Guezzam, a small village of no importance and with no petrol, on the actual border between Algeria and Niger, a large detachment of police, sub-machine guns and all, was waiting for them. The Scruffs were to be transported back to Tamanrasset where the carnet was waiting. When they arrived, the Algerian Government would pay petrol costs, and they were to drive their wrecked van back up the murderous Hoggar Trail, nearly 1,200 miles to Algiers, there to see the British consul. Bureaucratic cruelty and bloody indifference. And I know how sarcastic the consul, Mr Harcombe, would be, as he was to me. It was probable that any spirit in the Scruffs would be knocked out of them, and they would find it difficult ever to risk again.

Tonight I camped alone on hard clay, with Agadez roughly 110 miles away. I had made it on my own. It happened that the bed of sand where I was left by the English boys was the last impossible stretch for me to drive alone. Luck again. And despite the leak, Alexa is running well. I have opened my last packet of cigarettes, an English brand, which I had been saving for a serious bribe, and I feel content.

But something should be said about water here. Of course, it is scarce in the desert, yet having no water has a curious effect. For the hour this morning when I had none, I was almost completely detached with fear. When I filled up at the well, dirty, gob-polluted water that it was, the fear disappeared without even a residual taste. One lives so much for each moment, except now, at night. Now I can think of Fiona, of these words to be written and sent off (are they being published? I don't know. I just write and post them off. Will someone read them?) I think of my parents and the friends I must write to.

The Swedish-German-French safari is camped five miles away. A Swede has just driven up and said he had shot a gazelle, and asked me if I had any cooking oil. He could see my mess-tin with soup and stale bread cooking on my Primus next to me. I said I hadn't any oil, and he drove off. A lovely fellow.

December 14th, Agadez

This morning I managed to wash as well as shave, wasting water on the luxury. I thought I had enough and to spare. The car started immediately. I ate a huge bowl of porridge, and was on the road by 7.30. Five miles later the safari camp appeared. I waved, though with reservations and thoughts of their stomachs full of gazelle, but then I thought of being in Agadez tonight.

All went well for three hours. The track was rough, certainly, but there was no sand. Then I felt something was wrong, stopped at once and checked out the engine. The radiator was leaking again. With my large kettle, my tea-pot and a flask, I collected the water from the drain-pipe and examined the rubber seal. It was loose. While taking out the radiator, the safari drove up. One of the Swedes had sealing paste, which he gave me, and we lighted pipes and cigarettes and talked while waiting for it to dry.

But I was impatient. First, I now have a horror of holding anyone else up. Second, I wanted to make Agadez by nightfall, and cannot drive in the dark because both head-lights have fallen out and smashed. I said they should not wait for me, and they drove off. They asked if I had enough water. I said I had.

As soon as they had driven off I examined the seal. It would take another two hours to dry. Yesterday, I had fixed a rubber seal which lasted 24 hours. That was good enough; I could get it really fixed in Agadez. I fitted another rubber patch over the leak, which came from a loose stud at the bottom of the radiator. When I filled it up with water, it looked fine.

About 45 miles west of Agadez, the track forks. I came down one of the branches of the fork, and passed a water-hole, crowded with camels and donkeys, with people wrapped up against the sun dotted like colourful sacking amongst the animals. I did not stop. Everything was fine, the engine running smoothly, and I should have been in Agadez by 4 o'clock in the afternoon. At 2.30 there was a hissing noise again, and I found that the battering of the trail had re-opened the leak. Desperately impatient, I did not take the radiator out to fix it, but poured in sealing and more water, and drove on. By 3.30 I felt I was near to town when power was lost completely and the car stopped.

I had no more water. I knew the engine had been over-heating, but I thought that if someone came by with water, and I filled the radiator, it would be possible to drive on. Someone did come by, as I was on the last chapter of

L'Etranger, half an hour before darkness. He said Agadez was 4 miles away, gave me some water which I happily poured into the radiator, noting that it did not leak out very fast. I tried to start the engine. It would not go. After 4,300 miles of sweet running, I had pushed it too far. No one was to blame but myself.

At 7 o'clock, two Frenchmen, Bernard and Jose, came by in a Landrover, out of Tamanrasset the day before and bound for the Central African Republic. They towed me those last four miles, which is galling to think about.

Tonight I have a room at the Hotel de l'Air. It is expensive for me, £2 a room, £1 a meal, and even then I think the patron reduced his prices because of Alexa. I have tried the engine since I arrived. It still won't go. What is the matter with it? Still, soon I will eat again, real food, solid, you can feel it hit your stomach with a lovely thump. I can hardly wait. Tomorrow I will see what is wrong. Probably the head gasket has gone. That is fine; I have two to spare. I will also have the radiator fixed here, and Bernard tells me there is a mechanic in town.

It makes me uneasy, though, not to have the car running. It is like being stuck in the sand in the dark. I know I can fix everything tomorrow. Yet if a piston has gone? It is no use, just idle speculation. I am going to eat now, and will think of England with cold winds and fires and Christmas coming, wet streets with lights shining brilliantly, shopping, stamping feet, nostalgia. Here the sun shines and I am sun-burnt, but I am not at home.

December 15 - 16, static in Agadez

The rings on at least two pistons have gone. I am sure of it. At the moment, the car is with a mechanic having the valves ground thoroughly. We will see tonight if I can continue to Kano. There, they should have rings which I can make fit. Here there are none. I may have to hitch to Kano for rings. Whatever, I will not be stopped. But I must catch the weekly post here tonight, and I won't be able to say whether the car will be able to leave until tomorrow. Sitting here, not knowing, I feel rather helpless.

Yesterday I had the radiator repaired. It cost me £2, but the black mechanic made a strong job of it *(in fact he botched it with heaps of solder, and it was soon malfunctioning again)*. Throughout the morning I felt a strange lassitude, and it was not until mid-day that I looked at Alexa. I had been to see the customs men, but it was Sunday and everything official was closed. Barnard, the Frenchman who towed me into town, looked at the car. I removed the head and changed the gasket, yet when everything was fitted there was no compression. We lifted the head a second time and gave each valve 10 minutes work with a screwdriver and a small hammer. The head went on a second time, still no compression. It must be the rings.

As soon as I knew, even though it was bad, I felt relieved. There is a French mechanic called Jean Boudon in town, who owns the second hotel, *The Family House*. I saw him this morning. At a killing price, he is now working on the car, re-grinding valve surfaces on his machines. I am also staying the night at his hotel, as I must to get the job done. It costs less than the other, includes a shower in the room, and the meals also cost less. The dining room is not so grand, though. At the *Hotel de l'Air*, I felt part of the film set to South Pacific, with a beautiful dark-haired girl behind the bar, the owner in shorts restraining his tanned bellying body, fans turning in the ceiling, astronomical prices of beer, mud walls and rough log beams, pictures of racy expensive cars and faraway places over the liquor bottles. To complete the impression, the girl fetched a baby, hauled out a breast, and fed it serenely on the porch while watching us all work on Alexa. This second hotel is much quieter, but has a cinema at the back. From remarks overheard, it appears the two owners are deadly rivals, ready to cut each other's throats at the drop of a hat.

News, a small happy ray in the general gloom. I have heard by trail gossip of the Cowboys again. I met them in Morocco, delighting each village with their impressions of motor-cycle Hell's Angels. There were five, three Canadians, two English. After I entered Algeria, I heard nothing of them. But a party of white hunters – led by a strange detached man right out of a Hemingway short story – 38 years old but looks 26 – met three Canadians on motor-cycles at In Salah. The hunter said he had brought their luggage to Agadez. They must be the Cowboys, but what has happened to the English ones? There are two motor-cycles, one with a sidecar, and that is all I learned. They should be in Tamanrasset by now. Perhaps I will see them soon?

Claude, the Frenchman with toothache in Tam, managed to buy a lift through to Agadez. He is an orphan, and wants to work in Central Africa. In his pocket are $9, he has a bag of clothes and a sleeping bag; in the world, this is all he has. He was once a student, but as education costs money, he has to find work. I have a loaded car, but if the route to Zinder and tarmac again is as sandy as the last 500 miles, I may be able to squeeze Claude in. I must ask the police about road conditions. Claude is in a rough situation.

If everything is fine with the car tonight, and I can get away without spending more than $30, I should be on tarmac within 4 days. I am looking forward to it. Siafu Safari, that group of six English Landrovers, seems to have vanished. No one has heard of them. They said they would spend Christmas in Kano, and I wanted to spend it with them. There must be a party to celebrate this crossing. After that it is east to Chad, and down to the Congo. I am told the roads are very bad, but they have to be taken. There is only one route through to East Africa. I have no choice. All the words I hear about the car and me, admiring the crossing, are really not deserved. After making the choice to set out, and having set out, I am left with no choice but to continue.

December 17th

It was not the rings after all, but the valves. Monsieur Boudon, the mechanic, did a meticulous job on them, and we both burst into smiles when the engine started again. He charged me less than I expected; that is, his bill was £12, but when I gave him $30, expecting small change, he looked away and then gave me back half my money. I have not fathomed why.

There is a road of 300 miles, very difficult according to reports, between Agadez and Zinder. After that the tarmac starts, down to Kano, Nigeria, and then east to Maiduguri. I can say when those 300 miles are done that I have crossed the Sahara Desert in a 1937 Austin 7; it will wipe out old guilts. In all, the trail covers 1,500 miles. I thought the section from Tam to here was the hardest, but I am told there are 70 miles of deep, soft sand ahead of me. Claude, the hitch-hiker going to the Central African Republic with a philosophy of "quitte ou double" – which for him means find work or die – will be coming with me to Zinder. From there, I go south while he goes east.

December 18th. Morning, 33 miles south of Agadez

We camped before the sun set, having left yesterday evening. I wanted to get away from town. It was too easy to spend money there. Today there are the celebrations for 10 years of Niger's independence. It would have been nice to see it all, the fete, processions, wild music, dancing through the night, but I must make Kano by Christmas. So here we are. The road has been fine so far. There have been undulations, layers of hard clay spaced with ribs two feet apart, lying across the road, for mile after mile, shaking the car so that it is gradually falling to pieces. But I can swear quite well now, and otherwise I pick up relatively smooth surface by driving half on, half off, the main track.

I have run out of porridge, Claude is cleaning the breakfast cups, coffee only this morning, plus three boiled eggs, one of them rotten, which I threw away. The countryside is changing. Before there were stunted trees, grass like the down on a bald man's head, a few mud huts, and the people were mainly nomadic, clustered with their transport around each well. Now there are villages, huts of grass, even a western-looking building, fewer Arabs, more Negroes, more animals, and things that crawl over sleeping bags at night. Life!

I listened in the middle of the night to the radiator leaking. Both bolts holding it to the chassis had come loose, and I have lost water. After it was mended in Agadez, I felt I would be safe for this part of the journey. I won't be. There is water and to spare just now, but if the leak gets worse it could be dangerous. Water is normally something I let down the plug-hole after a bath at home. Here it is always in the back of my mind, pushing me under the bonnet time and again, to check how much the car is drinking. I conserve the small supply I drink each day until it is certain a well can be reached.

Driving with Claude, I find myself irritable. When alone, I had leaned out of the window and shaken my fist, cursing the builders, the government of Niger, history, the wind. Afterwards, I forgot about the difficulties because there was no object I could focus on to project my violence. The difficulties were just there to be endured. Now I find I turn all my resentment at the shocking road surfaces at Claude, if I do not make the conscious effort to keep things in perspective. It is not his fault that I am here. Certainly, he adds weight to the car, more than I have carried so far on the trip, but he will compensate by leaping out and pushing – that vital extra power – when Alexa sticks in the sand. Poor chap. I would find it difficult with my French to even explain what I am writing about him. Must be off now.

5pm, December 18th, 121 miles south of Agadez

I am still 160 miles from tarmac, but the half-shaft has gone. That seems to be it. I am finished.

Revving through a bank of deep sand, with soft sloping sides, there was a loud thump, the car slewed and then stopped. Claude jumped out and pushed, and I gunned the engine. It would not budge. I had heard a noise like that thump before, in Algiers, when the half-shaft of the Landrover went.

"The rear wheel isn't turning," Claude said.

"Sand-mats?"

They didn't work, the wheel just would not move. I walked around the car three times and thought of my two spare springs, and no spare half-shaft. The sun was going down in a red and black blaze through some clouds over a flat calm countryside.

"This isn't possible. This can't just be it!" I said in English.

Claude sat down and said nothing. I had been saving one English cigarette for Kano. That seemed absurd, so I lit it and thought.

"A half-shaft. I was told they wouldn't go. Hah! But why here?" I muttered.

If a truck came along, I blocked the road. It would be able to pick up my car, I reasoned. How much would it cost to have her carried to Zinder? What then? Perhaps another half-shaft cut on machinery? I hate Niger. What rotten luck. I finished my cigarette and paced around the car again. Claude sat in the sand and looked at the back wheels.

"Better take a photograph," I said.

He took one, both car doors open, rear axle buried in the sand, and I felt bitter when the camera clicked. Afterwards, I pulled out my Primus stove and lit up, putting a kettle on to boil. We started to make camp, fetching sleeping bags, food buckets, some dry bread, a tin of sardines, my emergency supplies. I thought we should feast, gorge ourselves, belch, sleep, and maybe it would not be so bad in the morning. But I have been honest with myself all this trip, and I know the situation will get better only if I make it better. Both of us watched the kettle, waiting for it to boil. It took ages. I started pacing again.

It isn't possible, it isn't possible, I muttered. Yet at first I felt strangely relieved, as if responsibility were lifted from me. I went through some of the motions of despair, pacing up and down, shaking my head, repeating inane little protestations, but underneath, for a while, I felt nothing.

What to do? What to do? Maybe I will make Johannesburg in time for Christmas? How? Sell the car? No! I would burn

her. Sell the typewriter, OK, I would get a good price for
that. Anything I was not offered a good price for I would
cold-bloodedly burn. Then Kano, buy a ticket to Zambia, bus
from there. Images of the bus journey, Fiona waiting,
stepping off and say, "hello, but I didn't make it". Marriage
with that bitter knowledge for the rest of my life. What
about the *Irish Independent?* That took a risk, taking articles.
Ah, yes. We both knew about that, me and the Editor and I'm
sure he would be pretty good. The readers might be
something else. Those who would say, "I knew he wouldn't
make it in a car that old". Floods of bitterness, another
cigarette. How dare they say that! If they took chances, fine,
they have the right. But not at home in an armchair with a
fire lit and a job to go to tomorrow, oh no. Still, I cannot do
anything about those people.

Parents? My father spent the last days before I left
planning a course of action if I failed to make it through the
desert. I told him I would take a truck and have the car
carried across, knowing I would attempt the drive. What
arrogance! If I had done that I would not be here with a
useless piece of machinery and not enough money to make
it to Joburg. But there are no Ifs. There is only what to do
now. I am here. Fine. What to do?

"I'll burn the car, you know, Claude", I said, but I knew I
couldn't do that.

I began to bargain in my mind. How much would I get for
the typewriter? I was offered £40 in Agadez. What about
the food? Ham, and they are Muslims here, so no luck, but
perhaps a European would take it? Two pounds of ham
won't fetch much. There is my watch. Cost me £4, worth
much more, especially here. I won't part with my Dunhill
lighter. Yet I will, if I have to. Do I have to? Face it, idiot,
yes! Clothes, how much for those? Not much. Will there be
enough to get a plane ticket? I did not know. I began to sell,
and was facing down the sarcasm of the various buyers for
the car, holding out for £200, when Claude said, "let us push
her again?"

"The half-shaft has gone," I said, walking towards the car

and touching a wheel. "I have heard that noise before."

"Let us push."

The motor started sweetly. If it was only that, I thought, stepping in and pushing into first gear. Claude pushed, I gunned the engine, there was a slight lurch and we started to move.

"Is the left wheel turning?" I yelled, like an idiot.

"Yes!"

I drove up a small ridge, parked the car, leapt out and hugged Claude. We both roared and laughed. We made promises of what care we would take, smoked seven cigarettes, ate a large meaty soup and lay on our backs for an hour, looking at the starry black sky. Later, I walked back with a spade, looked at the disturbed sand where the car had stuck, dug a hole in the road and carefully defecated. Justice. Even self-expression.

December 19-20th, 247 miles in two days

After the tearing anxiety of a suspected broken half-shaft, the rest of the journey to Zinder seemed easy. All through the 19th, we kept off the official track, making our way through light thorny trees, always heading south. Claude favoured riding with the door open, his feet on the running board, ready to leap out and push the car through soft patches. Once, Alexa stuck completely in a deep sandy patch during a rare venture back on to the track, and we spent half an hour digging and pulling the car backwards to get clear. At Tanout, the sand stopped. From there, corrugations were the only trouble. We filled up with water, bought more eggs, some of them rotten, and camped 60 miles from Zinder and tarmac. That night I broke open a tin of stew and we feasted royally.

Midday exactly on December 20th, with 34,846 miles on the clock, tarmac started again. I wanted to take a photograph, to compare Alexa's condition after 1,557 miles of Sahara trail, with the photo I took as we entered the desert, but the camera had stopped working. Then,

December 2nd, Alexa was pretty, in one solid piece, carrying
a roof rack, and she ran like a bird. The Sahara mounted up
an impressive score. It shook out both headlights, punctured
one tyre (I was lucky with tyres), loosened both front wings
so they now flap in the wind, knocked out the rear window,
clogged up and shorted the starter motor, ripped away the
wiring on the rear lamps, and hollowed out the valve
seatings. My nylon rope, envy of everyone, was stolen by
some Arabs, along with a blue nylon shirt, and my
sunglasses, hat, tyre pressure gauge, cylinder head spanner
and various useful pieces of canvas were mislaid. I jettisoned
two petrol cans and the roof-rack, after it had torn away the
rain beading south of Tamanrasset.

Claude and I parted company at Zinder. I drove like a
madman on smooth roads, reaching Nigeria by 4.30pm, and
smiling at the Guinness advertisement, featuring two huge
black smiling faces with the blurb in English, as I crossed the
border. I tried to celebrate by drinking beer alone when I
camped that night, but it was not a success. Drinking alone
never is. Anyway, I felt no triumph. The radiator still leaked,
the car looked a wreck, and I knew I was soon going to have
a money problem. What had happened to the triumph?
Before I started, the journey across the Sahara had been the
prime cause of all my nightmares. Now the Congo looms,
huge and unknown, while behind me the desert and all its
dangers seemed just troublesome, no more. I did sing once,
joy at the roads, then ran out of energy and stopped. Now I
don't feel like talking about it anymore, except for advice to
people who are about to start out on the trip.

 **CHAPTER 9**
Nigeria

The AA *guide said Nigeria was a Commonwealth country, its titular head Queen Elizabeth, and the population was 35 million. Its capital was Lagos, and its language English. The south is hot and humid, and rainfall is especially heavy in the south-east. The climate in the north – where I planned to stay – was warmer and less humid. In population terms, Nigeria was the biggest country in Africa, mainly agricultural, but with some industry in the south. There were all-weather roads between all the major centres, with 5,000 miles of tarmac.*

(What the guide didn't say, but which soon became obvious, is that there was a civil war going on inside Nigeria, mainly in the north between the Hausas and Yorubas, who populated the north and south-west, against the Ibos, who were a clever tribe with some of the survival qualities of the Jews and who lived in the south-east. As the influence and power of the departing British colonial era faded, Nigeria was already showing signs of that deep official corruption that now mark it as one of the most venal nations on earth).

The road south from Zinder to Kano, 196 miles, was tarmac, as was the 224 miles east to Maiduguri. Entering Cameroon, another deeply corrupt country, and almost immediately afterwards entering Fort Lamy in Chad, the track reverted to a bush trail, full of dust and drifts. According to the AA guide, the stretch from

Author, 25 years old in Fairholme Rd, West Kensington where he lived in a bed-sitter in 1966/7.

1967, Spring, Author and girlfriend Fiona Campbell, posing their noses together.

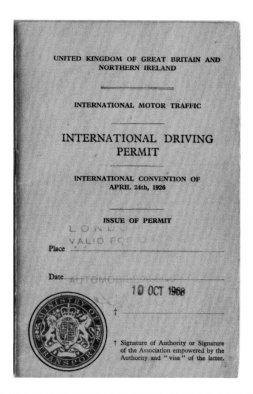

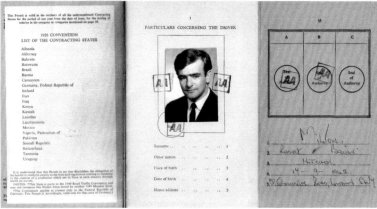

International driving license - hard to believe that was once me.

France - Siafu Safari, grossly overloaded before the journey's attrition had any effect.

November 22, 1968 - Spain. Tom Pearson with his ex-army truck in Algeciras campsite after tuning Alexa for thirty shillings.

November 22, 1968. Alexa minus roof rack but clean, hopeful and determined in Spanish campsite. Last full day in Spain.

Author and Alexa in Algeciras November 23, 1968. Prior to catching the "Virgin of Spain" to Africa.

Algeria November 25, 1968. On the coast road to Algiers, Alexa in all her travelling glory, no apparent damage.

Algeria, December 5, 1968 - In the Sahara between In Salah and Tamanrasset, note headlights going cross-eyed.

December 10, 1968. Sahara, Algeria - the campsite in Tamanrasset with the "Scruffs".

Sahara 1968, December 12. After pushing Alexa out of the sand, thus saving my life, both Arabs stole various items including my tow rope.

Niger - 5pm December 18, 1968 121 miles south of
Agadez. Author pissed off thinking the journey was over
because of a broken half shaft.

Nigeria - Hotel De France Kano, December 30, 1968. Hans,
Jackie, Author and Arthur, before Jackie flew home to
England.

In the Sahara. Paul Stott, one of the "Cowboys". Later
went down with Malaria.

Chad, January 11, 1969. Burning the broken Citroen Safari.
Arthur was "unapproachable".

Citroen Burning. Another view in No Mans Land between
Chad and C.A.R.

C.A.R. Arthur Lang, Werner Strieff and Vera Haldane on
the terrace of the main hotel in Bangui. The two men in the
background are thought to be french mercenaries.

January 21, 1969 leaving C.A.R. in a packed ferry to cross Ubangi River into Congo and Zongo catholic mission.

C.A.R. January 1969, lined up for ferry to cross Ubangi River to Congo. Unfortunate moment for Ursula.

January 27, 1969. Arthur Laug on air field near Kota-Koli mission in northern Congo where he fixed earth-movers and tractors and was treated as a god.

Congo - January 27, 1969. Captain Gaston Bebronne in Kota-Koli mission, by Derek Haldane's Landrover. He threatened to kill me - after a solo bottle of whisky - if I burned Alexa.

Congo January 29, 1969. At Kota-Koli mission, including
Author, Ursula, Arthur behind her, Mike half- hidden behind
him. Missionaries survived Simba killers 4 years earlier.

Alexa's engine in the Congo covered in oil with
modifications. Note no plug in the first cylinder.

January 31, 1969, heading for the Congo River. Meinhart Wagenshein with his 2CV after a brakeless Alexa dived into a trough.

Congo February 3, 1969, on the way to Buta. Werner and Arthur using Primus stove to solder radiator.

Alexa in Buta, Congo, empty headlights. Near the end.

Congo, February 7, 1969. Last day on the trail, 20 miles from Mungbere and down to two pistons. Tropical rain coming, aircraft circling.

Congo, February 8, 1969. Arthur with overloaded Citroen ahead of a 2-hour struggle across liquid mud to get to the photographer. Note pygmy on Arthur's left.

February 8, 1969. Last night in the Congo on border with Uganda. Barefoot, newly-washed and slim - Arthur, Author, Werner.

Fiona Campbell after we were married.

Dikwa, 56 miles east of Maiduguri, 90 miles through to Fort Lamy, may become impassable for days at a time during the rainy season between June and November.

Nigeria - December 20, 1968 - January 2, 1969.
34,930 - 35,526 (586 miles)
4,710 - 5,296 miles from London

A bridge was blocked on the road to Kano. I had heard about it at the border the day before. It should have been cleared by the morning of the 21st, but when I arrived there was still a huge and vocal debate on the best method of removing a wrecked truck from the bridge. Traffic was piled up a mile long on either side. At the block, a series of frenzied orders was given by everyone to everyone else, a truck was brought, a tow-rope attached, and about a hundred people helped to pull the wreck backwards from the bridge. The wreck went in one direction, the tow-truck in another, at a tangent. There was another frenzied burst of orders, the tow-truck stopped, and everyone pushed the wreck, rocking it on its wheels without much success, in an attempt to point it in the right direction.

It had apparently taken fifteen hours to decide on action, and it took three hours to remove the wreck and topple it into the river. It was only a small bridge. I felt like helping, or offering advice, but I did not know how they would feel after eight years of independence about a white man giving orders again. I found out later that the ghosts of Captain Kettle and Saunders of the River are still abroad in this land.

Leaking water from the radiator, the back window rattling on the petrol cans, covered in dust, the headlights like two sightless eyes dangling on the wings, I entered Kano at 12.30pm, and drove to the cheapest white hotel in town, the *Hotel de France*. On the shabby dining terrace four English people were eating lunch. One was Peter Hartnell, a chap I had known vaguely at school. It seemed normal. I was back in British territory. We talked about what each of us was doing. He taught in Nigeria. In the afternoon I went swimming in the Kano Club, took a week's membership, and by evening I was fully integrated and finding out who was who. Next morning the first symptoms of a curious lethargy set in....

There was a Christmas party at the Kano Club the night I arrived. Just to describe it is to describe one facet of this society. We walked off a dusty native street, past a cinema and a squash court, to face a large black man in a white coat with sergeant's stripes on his arms. He was strict about membership. Peter, my school friend, knew someone in the club, and after a short wait we were signed in. The man who endorsed us wore white shorts, white knee-length socks and a white shirt. Behind him, drinking, with those curious insensitive red faces of the British abroad, sat three men, watching the door. One was club president, a Mr Morgan. Feeling scruffy in my old jeans, and just off the desert, I changed for a swim, re-adjusting myself unconsciously. There were obviously all the old written and unwritten rules, and probably some new ones, in Kano, and as an Englishman I would have to know them immediately.

Swimming, sunning ourselves, watching other people, we talked. Peter had been there more than a year. One adjusts, he said. You try to talk to them as equals. They never reply in that fashion, or they become familiar. They always keep you in your place, on top. Soon you accept it. You are white, automatically you are rich. They are insulted if you tell them you are not rich. They call you Massa. But if you sit down and think about it, I said, no race is inherently master of another. Wait and see, said Peter.

At the dance I waited and watched. Lynn, a teacher there with VSO, like Peter and his two friends, came with us. She has specialised in Bertoldt Brecht, and I thought she would be an interesting guide, and her opinions might have some of that German writer's detachment. We sat at a round table by the swimming pool. There were coloured lights strung from poles, throwing the whole area around the pool into deep vague shadow. The bar near the door was crowded. By the middle of one long side of the pool, a stage had been set for band and record-players, then a space left clear for dancing, bounded on two sides by tightly packed tables, a candle on

each. The English sat on the right. On the left were the
Lebanese, with a few truly black people. Peter and Lynn and
me and two others, one called Paul, all of us white, were
isolated on the fringes of the latter. I did not mind, but it
struck me later that others might have.

Were we letting the side down?

There was music. It wasn't loud. For an hour I saw no one
dance. Once, three white men cavorted around the floor,
shouting and laughing. There were sporadic cheers, and
clapping when they had finished. Probably a bet settled. We
all drank. Talk hummed around us. Each table was isolated
from the others, yet crushed together. I was fascinated.

Later, I danced with Lynn. From her, I learned how
seriously the social game was played. Money was not
everything, which was a surprise, though having lots of it
was useful, as it is anywhere. If one is British, launders one's
clothes (which must be of a reasonably conventional
pattern), if one shaves, has the right accent, and plays the
game well, one inherits the legend of the perfect colonial
British administrator, and one is immediately accepted.
Later, having taken advantage of all the situations to make
some quick money, one had real power. But a lot of power is
donated, gratis, to a white man. He is at the top, for he must
be conscious of his whiteness.

If this consciousness lapses, circumstances soon restore it.

The rich here are the Lebanese. They are obviously not
British, nor technically white. Some, I was told, are
acceptable as company. They were too rich to be cut in any
of the small and large ways one cuts Lebanese. But I was
told their names on my first day here. All the rest one says
hello to, or nods to, but it is best not to accept them, even
once, as equals. Lynn spent ten minutes asking timid
questions to herself after she had danced with a Lebanese.
Was it the right thing? Strictly speaking, she concluded, it
was not. We were instructed to say that one of us was about
to dance with her if a Lebanese asked her again. And if one
talks to them as equals, it is nearly impossible to get rid of
them. They hang around for hours, ignoring the small signs

you hang out saying you don't want them around. In the end the only way is to be brutally rude. Then they might go.

There were some black people at the dance who were not stewards. They mingled with the Lebanese. I could not tell, in the darkness, whether they were Hausa or Yoruba. The latter have decorative facial scars. It is less than a joke to say with certainty that there were no Ibos there. Everyone names the same surviving Ibos, perhaps a few more than the four I kept hearing about in this area.

The pecking order was complicated. As a group, wielding power with the calm certainty of Saunders of the River, the British held themselves aloof. They gave orders, joked, laughed, and sometimes indulged in a one-way exchange of friendly insults with black people, but from the impregnable tower of their racial consciousness. Americans had the same position as the British, though their self-certainty was based on money, and as a whole I thought they were less respected by the Nigerians. The British often spent a life in Nigeria before retiring to Hampshire to moan about the servant problem, while the Americans were always temporary. All the other nationalities, German, French, Swiss, accepted the kudos offered to white people with perhaps less aplomb than the British, and except among the highest echelons, there appeared to be no national in-fighting.

Partly because they were stuck in the middle, with every qualification for the highest social position except self-certainty, the Lebanese were the most energetic. Watching them bank their naked money – all money is naked here, in brown £1 notes, carried in huge casual stacks to and from banks – or laughing together and discussing business in their own groups, or driving big fat cars, they seem to have everything. Many of them were good-looking, well-dressed, full of a surface confidence, gobbling up life with an attractive energy. Yet their attitude to the British was pathetic. Why should they have kudos among themselves for each British "friend" they gain? Is it a desire to be near the appearance of power? The Lebanese waded through a social minefield to remain in British company, when the easiest solution would be to walk away with a shrug when they learned they were interfering with the carefully preserved profile of a British colonial gentleman. Perhaps they did not want to learn?

I did my best the other night to ignore a young, rich drunken Lebanese slobbering over our table, trying to start up a conversation, trying to buy us all a drink, using money in an insulting way as if it would solve our terrible silence. I thought, he must go after 10 minutes. He took an hour. Even then he was by my room as I went to bed, timidly hurt, saying, why didn't you come and have a drink with me? And, you are not my friend? Why are you not my friend? Why would he do this? I can do nothing for him here. I am passing through. But I am British, and that is that; I inherit his respect, though I do not deserve it.

But the white man and the Lebanese are both parasites and builders of this society. We existed and thrived in a sea of black Nigerians. We danced under coloured lights, served by busy deferential stewards who needed the job we gave them, next to a swimming pool. Jack London would have called us the Lords of Life, had he been looking in from the outside and heard an edited version of our conversations. There were, of course, black Lords here. They were in the army, in politics, in the civil service, and they drove cars. I could not even begin to fathom the cross currents and allegiances among them, but I had some small experience of their corruption. I wondered if my lethargy came from that?

Three days later, between Christmas and the New Year, I wrote an article for the *Irish Independent*, which I don't think was published, another snapshot on Nigeria....

Peter and Paul are outsiders. They are dandies. Peter comes from Rhodesia, Paul from Zambia. They are both white, have socially correct accents and education, and they both teach in Nigeria. Until the end of December they will both be in Kano, the – relatively – civilised centre of Northern Nigeria. Next month they will be banished to the bush, Peter to a village 25 miles away over a rough track, Paul to Birnin Kudu, 90 miles away. Their banishment comes after multiple sins against unwritten and generally unspoken laws. Perhaps after a certain time they will be allowed back to see if they have reformed themselves. After all, what use is punishment without the judge's secret glee afterwards, at the change produced in the victim?

But Peter and Paul are intelligent. Their education has changed the way they think, which it does not do to that many people. In general, they act upon what they think, rather than the way they are required and expected to act. It is true they cut their hair when the rumour they would be transferred to the bush became strong enough to worry them. Too late. Will they be able to maintain their quiet but fierce independence? I hope so.

Their view of Kano is rather different from most of the British here. After my abortive attempt at a celebration, drinking two beers alone at night when I reached tarmac again, I felt in need of something better. Peter and Paul provided it.

They turned up one afternoon in the courtyard of the Hotel de France to have lunch, and to look at the battered body of my little car, waiting for repairs. I had seen them at Lynn's house on my first evening in Kano. She told me about them, in a slightly prim voice, and they sounded interesting. Over lunch, we discussed Nigeria. Both were born in Africa, and have, despite their English public-school education, a remarkably enlightened view of all the troubles on this continent.

We started to drink the local brew, beer, after two thousand miles of former French territory and wine. Somehow the idea grew that I should be shown their view of the city of Kano. I had planned to clean the car, and had already stripped the engine. But being past the desert, a pub crawl seemed a perfect way of celebrating the fact. I changed my clothes, so as not to be put to shame by their immaculate Carnaby Street outfits, and in Paul's Citroen 2CV – called a Yoruba Car by the natives – we set off for the Pink Peacock, a bar in Saman Gari, the native quarter. White people can go there and slum, but there were none there when we arrived. We tried another place, the Tropical Gardens. It was pleasant sitting on the roof terrace, listening to the bongo band warm up. You are probably the third white man ever to enter this place, said Paul. I put down my third beer. Black people came over, walking loosely and clicking their fingers to the rhythms, and grinned pleasantly at us. The service was excellent. I went into a detached state, suspended my normal judgements and let the evening drift along.

Then we met Kingsley. What does he do? I asked later. Oh, he's a pimp. He can get you anything for a commission, said Peter. Kingsley stayed with us through another bar, and watched silently as we three talked Rhodesian and South African politics. I asked questions, but listened mostly. Later, Kingsley and I talked about the Nigerian Civil War. There seemed no end to the subjects we could talk about between the four of us.

Bar followed bar followed bar. Somewhere Mary appeared. Peter, Paul and Mary; I hugged the poor joke to myself. Mary is a whore. OK. What should I say? This is Nigeria. I had never been here before. For the first time I felt I had arrived in Africa. On the road there was only the road surface and small villages where I stopped to buy petrol and food before I drove on and camped, generally alone. But that night I arrived. Bar followed bar.

We talked out South Africa, and went on to literature. Mary brooded across the table. She wants to marry Paul, Peter whispered in my ear. Paul smiled gently and was very vague about her.

At midnight, I was tired. Let's go dancing, someone suggested. We went, entrance fee three shillings, to listen to four highlife bands, all of them mediocre. Peter started going mad and flinging money around like water. Each band came over and introduced themselves to us, as if we were agents. There was a courtyard with a raised dais in the middle and we sat near the stage where the band played, facing the dais. Overhead, it was a clear starlit night, except for a fine mist of sand ("coming from your bloody desert", said Peter), blown by a cold wind. Music pounded out into the night, not quite loud enough to drown out the bingo calls from a room on the second floor overlooking the courtyard: "sixty-six, clickety-click....leggggggs eleven!" I laughed. How pervasive our culture is.

In the middle of one band's stint, the dancehall manager came to the microphone. He announced that the assistant director of schools for the northern region of Nigeria was honouring us with his presence. The next ten minutes was filled with a good deal of enthusiastic flattery. Then the manager railed against those who were not heart and soul behind the "Keep Nigeria One" movement.

Terrible punishments were called down upon deviationists. I believe these threats were directed at our table, for Paul and I were talking together and not listening raptly. After nudges, we stopped talking and watched him. He carried on his threats for the next two minutes and then waddled away. The music continued. Peter paid for two more rounds of beer. It got very cold.

Finally I was able to stand up without feeling I had neglected to pay attention to everyone, and said I wanted to sleep. Paul drove me back to the hotel. I thanked him for the evening. Without him and Peter, that part of Nigeria would have been closed to me. I learned a few important things. Prices for a white man are higher than for a black man. You can buy anything, or anyone, in Nigeria. Except General Gowon, according to legend. Kingsley would sell anything for a price. Mary cost £1. That's what her illegitimate baby cost. How many more will she have at that price? And Saman Gari had been full of Ibos once. Biafra, what's left of it, is the Ibo breakaway state. Ibos were slaughtered, gutted, their intestines thrown into paper bags and fed to dogs, right in front of the Central Hotel, the best hotel here, now full of mercenary pilots who will fly the six MIG-17's up at the airport. But I met only Hausas and Yorubas. They were very pleasant to me.

In the morning, I noticed that the large birds I saw flapping around the dusty compound of my hotel were vultures. They were not as ugly as I had thought they would be. Their daily meal is the same as ours. They eat the insides, and we eat the meat, of the chickens that wail like cats each morning as they are chased by the cook for killing. It is our breakfast serenade. The menu at the hotel has not changed for 20 years; soup, omelette and salad, chicken and grease and chips, pineapple. Nigeria is nearly ten years old.

I posted a letter to Fiona at around this time, enclosing the desert articles, and told her I had had a presentiment that I would arrive in Johannesburg on February 13th, 1969.

Kano, December 30, 1968

The Austin agents in Kano gave me a free service. The chief engineer passed the poor sad wreckage of my car, three days

off the desert, on Christmas Eve, and left a message at the
hotel. He was very nice about it all, especially considering
the car's terrible condition. I drove out of his garage with a
new starter-switch, my back window glued back in, oil in all
the right places – the differential had been empty – and the
car cleaned. But because of the war, no sealed-beam
headlights are available. I will have to wait until Kampala, if
I ever reach there, for those.

News...Kano is the place where all the desert accounts are
settled. On Christmas Eve, a group of three men and two
women walked into the hotel, grumbling and snapping at the
stewards and brandishing a gin bottle. I was sitting on the
terrace in my three-piece suit, waiting to be taken for a
Christmas drink by the Austin manager, who, through a sad
mistake, drove away without me. After a while, I asked the
group if they had come off the desert. They had, and who
was I? I said I had just come off the desert too, in an Austin
7. Is that so? they said, very interested.

"We've heard about you, but we thought you were dead."

The group were survivors of a Swiss Safari, six men who
had set off from Zurich in two well-equipped Citroens. Both
girls were Americans, and turned out to be those I had been
told about by a motor-cyclist called Ian, just after I had
entered the desert. There was a third girl called Jackie, at
present in a convent, waiting to be repatriated.

Arthur Lang, dark-skinned with short black hair and a
Ghengis Khan moustache and the fiercest drinker, told me
what had happened to their safari. They passed through
Europe and North Africa easily enough, taking the route south
of Oran and cutting across from Reggane to In Salah and the
Hoggar Trail, down which I had come. In the early stages of
the desert, they found a Thames van with a remarkable
Englishman called Roger Phelps in it, bound for South Africa.
They had virtually pushed Roger across the entire desert. He
sounded like a comic-book Englishman, and seemed to have
paid for their help by charming them. Often, said Arthur, when
they all leapt out to push Roger's van, and wondered where
Roger was, they found him in the front seat with a small stove

between his knees, brewing up a mug of tea.

The safari found the three girls – Karen, Marilyn and Jackie – at Tamanrasset. It was decided they should be given a lift to Kano, and both Citroens and Roger's Thames van set off south. After a relatively mild amount of trouble, the Nigerian border was reached, and soon afterwards they were stopped by a civilian who asked to look at their passports. One of the Swiss called Freddie Hunziger was irritated at this demand, and asked to see the man's own credentials. The man said he was a policeman, but he had no identification on him, so Freddie told him to go away.

About an hour later they were overtaken and stopped by two trucks and a car, and forty army soldiers and policemen surrounded them with guns. The civilian who had stopped them told them he had now found his credentials, and they would soon learn how people who did not respect the laws of a country at war were treated. They were escorted to a police compound in Kano and told to pitch camp. This was on December 10, the day I had left Tamanrasset. On Christmas Eve they were let out, £600 poorer than when they arrived.

Freddie Hunziger and Hans Schop, another Swiss, had gone down with jaundice and were sent back to Switzerland yesterday, which accounted for half the £600. The jaundice symptoms had been obvious for nearly a week, so Roger had decided to drive on alone. The other Swiss were seriously thinking of driving back home, their morale shot to hell, but one of them, Freddie Hammerle, had tried to reach South Africa in an earlier attempt, and he decided to go on in Roger's van. He was given £230 from the stake he had put into the safari. That left Arthur, Werner and Hans, plus the three girls.

The girls were a real complication. While in the police compound, an immigration officer for the city had visited them to check their credentials, and pronounced the Swiss responsible for the girls' welfare. This officer had once been to England, failed to find a job, and been repatriated. His position in an independent Nigeria gave him the power to work out his grudge, particularly on white people. He also wanted to go to bed with one of the American girls, which implicitly, it was gathered, would solve the problem.

The girl refused.

When I met them both girls were waiting for money to come through from the United States, Karen to get to London and find a job there, Marilyn to have enough to look around Kano and get a job as a nurse. The Swiss were going to blow all their spare cash getting drunk and buying souvenirs, then go back up the Hoggar Trail and home again. They had thought I was dead because they met the Landrover with the four English boys who had left me in the desert, and the boys had said I was probably dead by now. And that clutch which I had been told had broken was never fixed, because it was never broken. The Swiss said they had been rude to the English boys after hearing the story.

Jackie, magnificently cheerful, went home yesterday, with copies of all my desert articles which I felt I could not trust to Nigerian mails. Karen got her money, and the Swiss advanced £50 to Marilyn to enable her to stay and work, which she says she will mail to them *poste restante* in Nairobi. And because of Alexa, perhaps because of some help I gave them selling equipment, the three remaining Swiss have decided to escort me through to East Africa. I would pay them back from money I hoped I was earning from the *Irish Independent*.

The selling is an illustration of how some things work in Nigeria. It took a three-day wrangle to sell 8 good Landrover tyres, getting £52.10.0 after "dash", the word here for a lubricating bribe. At one time I had five prospective buyers, all, I am sure, who knew each other, each at one time saying £32 was his last price, "absolutely, sir!" Yet I know the tyres will fetch at least £13 each on the market. Someone tried to sell me a tyre for Alexa at £14!

Trying to sell one of the Citroens was very interesting. It was possible, said our smooth agent, nicknamed Fatty Two, but certain arrangements would have to be made about the carnet de passage at the Ministry of Trade. We went to see an official, with Fatty Two's blessing. The official spent the first half hour on a sincere explanation of the difficulties of selling a car in Nigeria. The next ninety minutes were filled with a passionate denunciation of the corruption of the Ibo tribe, inside as well as outside "so-called Biafra". He spoke in the same terms as a Nazi might use of a Jew.

"How corrupt the Ibos are, and what murders they will commit to achieve their ends," he said, again and again. "We will rid the country of these vermin and build One Nigeria".

It was all very fine and moving, even if Arthur, who was with me, could not understand what it had to do with selling his car. Justice, I was assured, would triumph over corruption. We found out afterwards why the official moved so restlessly every time he spoke. Our agent was aghast that we had not dashed him a fiver for the import licence. Corrupt Ibos indeed! In the end we could not find a way through the corruption to sell the Citroen – our asking price was £700 – and we planned to drive on with it.

December 30, Kano, preparing to leave

Yesterday a Landrover drove into the yard of the hotel, the only apparent survivor at present of that grandly-equipped group called Siafu Safari which I had been told to join by the British consul in Algiers. Derek Haldane, proclaiming his Scottishness with a rampant lion on his car door, brought his wife Vera and two others, Ursula Carmen, an Englishwoman, and Ray Saunders, the American I had liked in Algiers, who is normally an expatriate in Paris. Ray told a bitter tale about Snafu Safari, as he calls it (Snafu – Situation Normal, All Fouled Up).

After long delays, during which they were joined by Robert Auberson – the Swiss I had met at the campsite at the bottom of Spain – the safari left Algiers and headed south. Morale was reported to be very low. Bad driving broke two half-shafts per vehicle before Tamanrasset was reached. Food had been rotten, one near-mutiny had been averted by fast talking, and the leader, Tim Bailey, was criticised with every breath. Forgive my delight, but most of the safari had been condescending towards Alexa the night I met them, and I felt glad I was ahead of them and still going. When last heard of, the safari was stuck in Tam, held by the police for selling radios without an import licence to…the police. A truly African situation.

Derek survives. He will follow after us with Vera and Ursula, to meet us in Fort Lamy. Ray is joining the Swiss as a companion to Arthur in the second Swiss Citroen ID19. Ray may buy a 2CV in Chad and drive on independently. Another Citroen 2CV, driven by a huge German schoolteacher called Mike – Meinhard Wagenschein – came in with Derek, and will go on together with us to Chad.

And today, the Cowboys arrived. I had met them in Morocco, heard nothing of them through Algeria, small scraps of news through Niger, Derek reported them in Agadez selling their bikes, and today they arrived. Paul Stott, the leader, stood in the courtyard with his peeling red face and dirty white Aran smock, and we clapped each other on the back and shouted and were generally glad to see each other. With him were Brian, a Canadian, and Ian, the English mechanic whose idea it was originally to motor-cycle to South Africa. Peter and Bruce, the other two, got cold feet in Algiers, and took a boat to Italy to carry on touring Europe.

The Cowboys' tale is magnificent. They suffered broken wheels, sand storms, leaking petrol and water tanks, and one attack by Arabs who stole their food, cooking utensils and various useful pieces of equipment. When they arrived at Agadez, the Frenchmen who owned the hotels would not change their American money into Niger's currency unless they stayed at the hotels. This is a common complaint of travellers across the desert, but how else are the hoteliers to make their money than from us "tourists"? The Cowboys spent a miserable Christmas Day, eating dry loaves of bread, then sold their bikes to the sons of two rich locals, and legged it out of town before the bikes broke down. They bought a truck ride to Kano, and were chucked out of the Kano Club ("too scruffy") by Mr Morgan, the president, after they had gone there for a beer to wet their throats. I met them immediately afterwards.

I told Paul I would take him through to Kampala, but it was an impulsive decision. My money is running out. I had wired home for some, and waited a week, without luck. Paul could share expenses. Later, I changed my mind. I was worried about Alexa. There was another 2,000 miles of trail after Maiduguri in Eastern Nigeria, before East Africa, and with two people the car would not make it through to Uganda. Paul would not want any chance of being left in the Congo, because of its fearsome reputation. I felt pretty bad about the change of mind, and offered Paul a ride through to Maiduguri free. It was tarmac all the way. I think Paul had malaria anyway, and it looked like it was getting worse. The Swiss agreed to take Brian and Ian to Maiduguri to join Paul.

We were all glad to be leaving Kano. Only those who lived there could accept all its social nonsense. It could take us three days to get through to Fort Lamy, in Chad. From there, to Bangui in the Central African Republic, there were reports of a good trail. After that, Bangassou, and then the Congo. We all speculated about the Congo. Soon, I hoped, we would be there. I was still worried about my car, though. She was using more oil than usual, and though the tickover sounded fine, some odd noises crept in. When I reached Maiduguri the journey would be half over. I will have done 5,200 miles. Considering the terrain ahead, it was absurd that being halfway should comfort me, but it did.

I must finish packing the car. The hotel has been paid for. Werner says his Swiss safari will grubstake me through to Kampala. I asked the bank to forward money to me. We should leave by 4 o'clock this afternoon, and bring in the New Year – 1969 – on the road. As long as we got out of Kano, and all its expenses, then brought in the new year wherever we were, I would be happy.

(Much, much later, when it did not count anymore, I heard that my father, on receiving copies of my articles brought home by Jackie, phoned the Austin Motor Company. Lord Stokes had told me, before I had left England, that there was "no commercial interest" in my journey. But after the Sahara crossing, Austin's became keen enough

to send a representative up from Lagos to contact me. He arrived in
Kano on January 2, 1969, two days too late. I left Kano with $20 in
travellers cheques, in fief to the Swiss, and the rest follows...)

January 1/2, 1969, 330 miles,
Kano to trail east of Maiduguri

We made good time out of Kano. Paul weighed down the car
a little, but he was company, and with tarmac roads, I was
content. In two hours the car went 60 miles, but she ate rather
a lot of oil. New Year's Eve we camped by the side of the road.
It was a very sophisticated camp for me. The Swiss parked
their two cars back-to-back, put a table between, lowered four
chairs, dropped a kitchen unit and turned on an electric water
pump, drew lights from the battery to illuminate the whole
scene, and within 20 minutes we looked like a rich group of
tourists taking our leisured time through Africa. This was a
change from my small camp in the desert, a pot of soup, one
lonely sleeping bag and a hurricane lamp.

After supper, while fetching something from my bed,
donated by the Swiss, I heard a noise like rustling leaves. It
came from the ground, a huge column of ants marching on
my bedding; Arthur described it as a marabunta. I called the
others over and we shone our torches on the column, which
was strung-out but orderly, and definitely interested in my
bed. Terrific organisation. Perhaps we scared them, because
the column ground to a halt, turned about, and marched busily
back the way it had come, finally disappearing into a bush.

On New Year's Day I made a great daily distance for
Africa, 224 miles all the way to Maiduguri, including a stop
for a puncture. Paul felt worse and worse as the day went on.
Just as the sun was setting, four miles outside town, there
was a road-block manned by three drunken soldiers and one
sober policeman. The soldiers wanted some fun. Search the
cars from A to Z, they kept saying. In the end, the policeman
prevailed. With Werner and Hans lighting the way, for I had
no headlights, we managed to find the Lake Chad Club before
it was too dark.

The club was Maiduguri's equivalent of the Kano Club, a place where expatriate Englishmen got together and drank. But travellers were much rarer in Maiduguri, so we had a good welcome, despite our bohemian appearance. I was treated to a beer for Alexa's sake. Within 10 minutes there were 17 empty beer bottles lined up on the bar, and we were settling into an evening's serious bash. The Swiss drank lustily; we decided we could not be bothered to cook dinner, and ate steak and chips at the club, between drinks.

This morning, at 7.30am, Ray and I stumbled across the club grounds and dived into the swimming pool. It was marvellous. The air was cool, but the water was warm, and a shower afterwards, bliss. Kicking the Swiss out of their tents was fun. They lumbered around, groaning and muttering, reaching for cigarettes, unapproachable until after their porridge. Paul lay in his sleeping bag and couldn't move. He was really ill. I took him to hospital. It was probably malaria, worse than in Kano. The other two Cowboys, Brian and Ian, had breakfast with me.

The day dragged on. We had to get petrol, buy some food and think about the route we were going to take. Ray wanted to see a game park in the Cameroons called Waza. I was not at all keen, but we were heading for Fort Lamy afterwards, so an extra day would not hurt. I had the punctured tyre mended by some ham-fisted mechanics who took two hours over the job, and this afternoon we managed to get away. We left the Cowboys behind, but they had enough money and should be fine. Ian was offered a job, admittedly at 1130 the previous evening when there wasn't a sober breath drawn at the bar, at £2,500 a year as a motor mechanic. He is worth it, especially out here. The black Nigerians are pretty good at simple jobs on an engine, like filling it up with oil, for example, but let them fit a new set of pistons, or tune a carburettor, and you have had it.

I drank in the last 40 miles of tarmac, poignantly aware of the 2,000 miles of *piste* ahead. The car felt fine, light after Paul's weight. At 3.33 pm, on January 2nd, with 35,456 miles on the clock, the car crossed a bridge and we entered washboard conditions again. I felt miserable. I had to wait half an hour for the two Swiss Citroens, and I sat and wondered if Alexa would not survive. Luck. I had a feeling I was relying too much on it. We will see.

The Citroens arrived, Arthur at the wheel of one with his elbow out, Ray sitting on the roof, then Hans at the wheel of the other, with Werner sitting back in dark glasses and his characteristic blank face, which glows when he smiles. Leading the way I lost my map, which did not seem to matter, but somewhere just west of the Cameroons the track forked, and we spent an hour driving in the wrong direction. Finally, heading the right way again, periodically stopping for self-important police checks, we wallowed through a huge bed of dust and camped just on the other side.

We ate well. Ray is a fine cook. He takes his time and fusses over the food, but when it is finished, it's delicious. Afterwards, burping away heartily, smoking, looking at the sky, we thought ourselves lucky to be leaving Nigeria. Hans went pottering around and then shouted excitedly. He had found two pens in the dust by one of the Citroens that could only have belonged to Freddy Hammerle, the Swiss who had gone on with Roger Phelps, two weeks ahead of us. They must have camped in exactly the same place. Had they been lost too? Did they camp, as we camped, just before the sun had gone down? Any article one leaves lying around, even for a second, is liable to be stolen. The pens had been at least 10 days in the dust, and of all people to find them, us!

At midnight, sleeping, Arthur woke me. Behind him was a soldier with a rifle. Bloody Nigerians again. We might, they said, be mercenaries. Was the white cross on the red background anything to do with Red Cross relief to Biafra? No, we said acidly, it was the flag of Switzerland, which is a neutral country. It was the sixth time that day we had been checked. Once the same group of soldiers gave us two goings-over, once in one sector, and when we moved on to the next sector, once there too. Bureaucratic idiots.

 CHAPTER 10
Cameroon

The AA guide described Cameroon as a republic, with a population of 4 million, its capital Yaounde. Its main language was French, though English is used in the former British Cameroon, now the western region. The coastal areas are always hot, but it was cool at times in the interior. There were said to be all-weather roads going down to the Congo, but we never found them. It was heading towards the position of being the most corrupt country in the world

January 3/4, 1969. 35,516 - 35,670 (154 miles)
5,296 - 5,450 miles from London

Into Cameroon next day, with relief, at 1015 in the morning. The *piste* was choked full of dust, from Mora to the game reserve at Waza. Ray sat on the roof of Arthur's car and commented in the eternal wondering way he has about the countryside. I drove furiously, at last able to get up enough speed to float over the undulations. But I resented this side trip to the park. It would be fine if I was not keen on getting past the Congo down to Johannesburg and marrying, if I was not driving Alexa. When we reached a series of cols, each with a small hut on them, that was Waza, I was in a terrible black temper. Ray unfortunately took the brunt of it. I should not travel in company. I knew that before I started.

After the detour, we decided the park was too expensive for us, at £4 a head, plus the cost of a guide. We drank a couple of beers, camped under a high hill near the park in a full moon, and prepared dinner. A young African called Francois stood watching us for a while. Then he washed his hands and helped Ray to peel onions. He had been trained as a steward by a French family, who had returned home. We were just what he was looking for. That night, excellently-served food put us all in good humour. Francois wanted to come with us, wherever we were going. He would be worth his weight in gold in New York, except that after a while he would rightly ask why he should be a servant, and he would be no good as a steward after that.

Ray and I argued in the morning. We are different types. I am like a bear until after coffee, and then I worry about the car. Ray is up and singing like a lark, commenting on the morning, cheerful and bright. To me it is uncivilised to discuss John Wayne movies, and why I will not go and see one, at 7.30 in the morning. Ray felt differently.

Alexa's engine made a funny noise when I started it. After running for a while I thought I had made a mistake, but the drive north towards the road that leads to Fort Lamy confirmed my fears. I think a piston did go in the desert. The car used two litres of oil, or 4 1/2 pints, in 120 miles. That must mean the rings. We will have to stop in Fort Lamy and see what we can do. Arthur is a good mechanic. Perhaps something can be done. I don't think too much about it yet, until we strip the engine.

Camped tonight by a hotel, overlooking the River Chari and Fort Lamy. We have had a beer, it is becoming a habit with us, and Ray made a salad. The border guards in Chad gave us a hard time for two hours, just to get the carnets stamped. Fort Lamy looks rich, full of Frenchmen. Another independence day holiday is coming up. We are plagued by them. And the prices here are terrible. Beer costs eight shillings a bottle! We are talking again about selling the second Citroen.

 **CHAPTER 11**
Chad

Colonised by the French in the late nineteenth century, Chad is landlocked, and has an area of 495,000 square miles, dominated in the centre and west by Lake Chad, shared with three other countries, Nigeria, Niger and Cameroon. Chad is largely desert in the Arabic-speaking Muslim north, with few roads, and arable in the black Christian and animist south. When the AA guides were compiled in the late 1950's, the French organised travelling along well-maintained roads, but outside of the capital, Fort Lamy — now called N'Djamena — these roads were not made of tarmac. There was strong tension in early 1969 when I entered the country, resulting in a coup later that year. The two major languages were French and Arabic, the population mainly rural and illiterate, and the French still exercised control through its domination of the currency, the CFA.

January 4th - 12th, 1969. 35,670 - 36,081 (411 miles) 5,450 - 5,861 miles from London

We stayed at Fort Lamy for five nights. I was too depressed by Alexa's condition to keep a diary, or write articles. Most of the time, after stripping the engine and finding two rings had broken on number one piston, we spent swimming in the river. I had not, at that time, heard of bilharzia. The Chadians celebrated their holidays, and in between we found a Frenchman who would cut the pistons, so Renault Four rings could be fitted. I had no spare Austin 7 rings, another economy in England which cost so much more later. As the ledge between one ring and another on the broken piston was loose, we were pretty doubtful if any permanent fixing job could be done, but as always, I had to try.

Derek and Mike found us the ideal camping spot in a Catholic mission, with a pit to drive Alexa over for repairs. The weather was hot and dry. Arthur and I swam frequently, once borrowing a canoe and paddling upriver. Derek, Vera, Ursula and Mike went off for a day trip to Lake Chad and came back with whopping tales of crocodiles and Mike's leg being bitten, which I nearly believed but the cynical Swiss scoffed at. Ray was very unhappy, which I did nothing to alleviate. The Swiss did not want him anymore, because they were determined to get rid of their second car, and Derek would not take him back. He tried to buy a Citroen 2CV, but wrecks were being offered for £150 or more, which would not last ten miles.

At this point I had better collect together the names of what we were soon to call the Grauenhalf Safari. The word means "terrible" or "horrible" in German, and we were always saying it when things went wrong. The safari consisted of nine members originally, soon to be whittled away:

Derek and Vera Haldane – Scottish. He's a management consultant, she is a teacher. They left Scotland in a grandly-equipped Landrover to join the ill-fated Siafu Safari. Derek planned to make a film for Scottish Television, but his camera was stolen by Arabs. He is stuck with £300 worth of 16mm film stock, and nothing to use it on. Both plan to work for a year in South Africa, ship their Landrover to South America, and drive up the west coast to the United States.

Ursula Carmen – English. Ex-Siafu Safari, travelling with Derek. She says she owns an advertising agency in South Africa. She is the real tourist of the group, buying things, eternally curious, but she is quite self-sufficient, disappearing for hours on her own. A potterer. When we reach the Congo, we plan to put her in Mike's car to pose as his wife, to lessen her chances of being raped.

Meinhard Wagenschein ("Mike") – German, teacher of economics, drives a Citroen 2CV, originally alone. A huge fellow, 6ft 5 ins, terribly meticulous, a little like the German in *Those Magnificent Men in their Flying Machines*, with a book in one hand and a dismantled stove in the other. His lack of English tends to make him sound unsubtle. He is rather puritanical, thus our teasing him about Ursula as his wife. Earnest in expressing his opinions. Belongs to an organisation which is totally against war. Believes if everyone belonged there would be no more war. Would like to force everyone to belong.

Arthur Lang – Swiss, dark complexion, rumpled indecent black shorts with feet at 120 degrees to each other. Always chews a tooth-pick, laughs like a scrubbing brush, brilliant inventive mechanic, very steady temperament. A drinker of some note, but like the other Swiss, pines for a girl back home.

Werner Streiff – Swiss, safari treasurer. A little plump, with a usually expressionless face, cultivating a beard, very careful about money and the chances we have to take with rumours. Pines mightily for a girl back home, and is Arthur's oldest friend. An electronics engineer and electrician.

Hans Tanner – Swiss, youngest on the trip at 19, also has a face which he keeps absolutely expressionless, then suddenly grins like a child. He appeals to many of the girls we have seen, particularly at the Maiduguri Club, and also the pretty young black girls. He is keenest of the Swiss to get to South Africa. An electrician.

All the above are in their twenties, except Arthur, who is 30, and Ursula, who is of indeterminate age (possibly early 40's).

Ray Saunders – American, expatriate living in Paris, about 40 but young-looking with a sharp lively face and blonde crew-cut hair. Third survivor of Siafu Safari to date, but lost to us in Fort Lamy. In other circumstances I think we might have been friends. Last heard he was going sadly back to Paris, not to try this journey again.

On the 9th January we got our pistons back from the French engineer complete with new rings, and Arthur carefully fitted the connecting rods on to the crankshaft, closed up the engine, and prepared to run it again. The starter-motor packed up (never to run again, though we could never discover why), so we wound up the starter handle, and the engine sounded strong. We were ready to go again. In what remained of the day we covered 30 miles south, heading towards Bongor.

January 10th, 168 miles covered

It has been a difficult and interesting day. I thought twice the car was finished, and yet it isn't. Alexa is difficult to kill, to use Arthur's phrase.

After shaking off Fort Lamy, and a cold night with the mosquitoes coming out late and fooling me into thinking I did not need a net, we all leapt out of bed this morning, glad to be on the road again. Sitting in any place, waiting for repairs or visas or the hundred things we wait for, brings us down slowly. On the road we only have to worry about starting the cars. Mine started fine. All four pistons worked well. I was losing a little oil, but that, I thought, would stop, when the new pistons bedded themselves in. Despite being five cars, we managed to leave the site by 8 o'clock.

The road to Bangui, capital of the Central African Republic, follows the River Chari. We decided to keep to the west road, avoiding Fort Archambault. Bandits are reported near there. We cannot laugh at these reports. The struggle between black Africans with tribal religions, and Muslim Africans and Arabs, is getting very fierce. It is probably going to be a bother in the Congo, what with refugees, but let that wait.

What more can one say about the *piste* here? Washboard, dust, broken tarmac fifty years old, odd rocks. Add to that the animals that potter across it, small groups of people squatting for a chat, trucks with punctured tyres blocking the track. I killed a chicken this afternoon. It was my first. Arthur congratulated me afterwards. We would have stopped to pick it up after I ran it over, except the owner was fairly agitated about his loss. Sausage and mash this evening.

Alexa, though, gave us trouble. I started off leading the convoy, belting down the road with this morbid fear I have about holding people up. At about 10 o'clock, it was obvious I had lost power, so we stopped to look. There was oil all over the engine. Arthur listened, said the rings on number one piston had gone again. The pressure in the crankcase had sprayed oil all over the starter motor, which has not worked for the rest of the day.

I asked Arthur if it was all over. He shook his head. This was not very cheerful of him. I had at least to get the car to Bongor. My carnet de passage was signed into Chad. If it was not signed out, an insurance company in London would get a demand for import duty. So we pondered the engine for a while. Perhaps if we took off the lead between the distributor and the number one plug, it might be better? Mike and Derek went on ahead, promising to stop for lunch, so we could catch them. Then Werner and Hans went after them, leaving Arthur in his crippled second Citroen to look after me. The back axle bracket on his car is broken, I learned tonight, and needs welding, which we cannot do until we reach Bangui.

After removing the distributor lead, Alexa went better for a while, but oil was gushing from the filler cap, the starting handle and the cam-shaft securing bolt. I have only one gallon of oil in reserve. At 1130 I felt her losing power again, so we stopped.

"It is bad," said Arthur.

He went into one of his characteristic thinking fits. When he is like that, nothing else gets through to him. I wanted to go on, oil or no oil, but I was feeling distinctly pessimistic. Being with other cars does not bring home to me immediately that if Alexa breaks down, the trip, for me, is over. I thought about arriving in Johannesburg with the Swiss. It did not seem so bad. Alexa had crossed the Sahara, anyway, if she could not make it through the Congo.

"We should be taking the plug out," said Arthur. "Then the piston, he does not push out the oil, eh?"

We took the plug out. I have driven the rest of the day on three pistons. Funnily enough, the car went better this evening than it has done for some time. It was as if number one piston had always slowed us up, and now it is useless, my Austin 5.7 has enough power to make 35-40 mph still. I have told the others I may hold them back, but I will only abandon the car when it is really dead, and then I will burn her. Kampala is just 1,500 miles away *(if it had been, this would be a different story. The actual distance was 2,100 miles).* Derek says he will go on if I am too slow. Mike will probably go with him. The Swiss and I will make it together in our two crippled cars. We will stay together because the more I owed them, the stronger the reason was for them to get me through.

Camped tonight in a school yard, surrounded by roughly 300 young natives. Our cars are parked in a circle; we sit in the middle, me typing, the others playing with a tape-recorder. All the children have sung for us. Now they are listening to some music Derek had recorded in Scotland. They smell of earth and sweat, but they are vastly amused by us.

January 11/12, 229 miles covered

Now we have only one crippled car left, mine. The other one was burned yesterday.

It was a desperate decision. There had been a chance to sell the second Swiss car in Nigeria. We did not take it, put off by all the corrupt demands for money. The price offered was too low, and I was not sure the Nigerians would not play more legal games with us after we sold it. It is easy to be wise now, and say something is better than nothing. In Fort Lamy there was another chance of a buyer, but he did not come through. So we drove on. Arthur had the crippled car, and looked after me. In the end we worried about the expense, and it was decided that to survive with enough money, we had better destroy Arthur's car. I do not think the choice between burning Alexa, and burning his car, was ever consciously made. In any case, no mention of it was ever made to me.

After breaking camp yesterday in the school yard, and driving 30 miles, Arthur put his car into a piece of clear ground about 30 yards from the track, and we ripped it to bits. I took the headlights to fit on to Alexa in Kampala, plus a fire extinguisher. Derek pottered around picking up clips and tut-tutting all the time at the waste of a good vehicle. Arthur was unapproachable. He called us vultures, even though he had been a decision-maker, and he became a little hysterical. I set the car alight at 11.30 after Arthur and I had tossed petrol over the seat covers. Arthur tried to set it alight, but somehow was not able to do it, and he asked me to complete the job. The car took ten minutes to catch fire, then burst into flames. We drove off soon afterwards, following a cup of tea. Two Chadians were seen waiting for the flames to die down as we left.

At lunchtime, covered in dust, we drove in to Lai. Immediately, it had become a habit, the Swiss and I headed for the nearest bar. We talked to three Peace Corps volunteers who told us there was no petrol between Lai and the border, as Chad and the Central African Republic (CAR) were spoiling for a fight with each other, the premier of the CAR having called the premier of Chad a silly old woman. We did not have enough petrol to get into the CAR, but we had given up worrying about such things. Werner ordered four more beers. Something always turned up, we said, and drove on.

In the middle of the afternoon I had a puncture, just as I was waved down by the others for a swim. The river was shallow, only as deep as our waists in the middle, and fast-flowing. We wallowed around and played tag and washed ourselves. Sometimes we were really tourists. In the evening we found an American Protestant mission, and camped in its grounds. Dick, the missionary, was one of those nice Americans with blond hair and a shy manner and carbon-copy children. He was dedicating the rest of his life to spreading the gospel in these regions. I asked him about petrol. He had some, and sold us 10 gallons at par, which was very nice of him, for there was very little petrol in Chad, and you could ask what you liked for it. A visiting missionary, a New Zealander, talked to the others last night as I lay in bed. I was not very happy that he kept me awake. He told me this morning that he was lonely.

Today my car has been a perfect lame duck. It stopped five or six times, holding up the others for a total of four hours. There were no complaints. It is difficult to say how much of a relief it is that the others understand the car, and my attachment to it. This is especially true of Arthur, as the mechanic. I wallow away on the shocking *piste*, swearing healthily again, sometimes driving sideways to avoid the undulations, with the Citroen behind me. Now and again I peek in the mirror, needing the reassurance that it is still there. Each time I stopped, Arthur came over, grinning, a cigarette sticking out of his mini Genghis Khan moustache. He pokes the engine, twisting this and that, shouts at Werner, Werner joins him poking the engine, and I feel superfluous. There was water in the carburettor, mud in the water pump, the battery shorted on one of my spanners, the tool bag burst into flames, a spring on the accelerator broke and we secured it with a thick rubber band, and finally a connection between the condenser and the coil fell away. That was the score for the day. After the water in the engine, we heaved away at the starting handle, pushing the car a good quarter of a mile in efforts to start it, changed the plugs for luck, and in the end, success. Over a hundred miles covered today, which is not much for Derek and Mike.

CHAPTER 12
Central African Republic

The AA Guide said that the Central African Republic in 1960 was a republic, with a population of 1.25 million, and its capital is Bangui. It was a country with high temperatures throughout the year, but economically very poor, with no known mineral reserves. All-weather roads were alleged to connect CAR with Chad and Cameroon.

The guide did not say the country was run by a former sergeant in the French African forces called Bokassa, later known as Emperor Bokassa, who was said to eat children.

The roads were untarred, but considered generally all-weather, though there may be hold-ups in the summer season, from July to October. All rivers were bridged.

January 12 - 21. 36,081 -36,454 (373 miles)
5,861 - 6,234 miles from London

Getting into the CAR was a trial. When I reached the border post south of Gore, third in line after Derek and Mike, I was in a filthy temper. Every guard was drunk, and there were thirty or more of them. Derek, with Vera's help, was almost through the formalities, but my arrival threw the whole situation. We had to start all over again, passports, carnets, driving licences. First the chief said it was OK to go on, then he retired to the bar and the small-fry wanted to search for themselves, hoping for presents. Then the chief returned and there was utter chaos. Arthur talked to me soothingly, holding me in the car, saying it would not help to blow up. We went for a beer and treated the chief, which cooled me down, enough so I could manage a smile with my teeth when Arthur whispered fiercely that scowling was no use. We spent an hour at the whim of those drunks.

Camped tonight next to a village. Arthur is sure he sees ghosts, but each time we go out with a torch, we find only trees and shadows.

January 13/14, 292 miles covered

Werner was worried that the 13th would be unlucky for us. There were 460 kilometres between the village where we had camped on our first night in CAR, and Bangui, the capital, across the river from the Congo. I had breakfast early, and left without shaving. The situation had to be really serious for me to do that. My visa for the CAR was valid for 48 hours only, all I could get in London, and I needed an extension. Bangui was the only place to get it. Derek, Vera and Ursula had the same type of visa, and were also worried about it. We thought we should at least try to cover the 460 kilometres in one day. With luck, I might have done it. With a different type of luck, I didn't.

At first, it seemed it would be a dead day. The oil pressure went straight off the clock half an hour after I set off. That meant the oil jets were blocked, the same trouble I had in London when the big ends went. I cleaned the jets, and the others caught up with me. We drove on as fast as I could over the rotten *piste*. Soon, the engine over-heated. I stopped, looked, saw the water pump was leaking, water bubbling in the radiator, and the usual coat of oil that has been on the engine since I started running on 3 pistons was burned off. We tightened the bolts on the pump, Arthur went for water, and by 11 o'clock we had covered 56 miles in four and a half hours. Derek got impatient and drove his Landrover ahead of us into Bossangoa, where – we learned later – he ran into trouble at a police post. He waited for us, worrying about his visas, and drove the remaining 200 miles into Bangui in the afternoon. Meanwhile about an hour behind him at one time, we bowled into Bossangoa.

This was where the good luck stopped us. I was first in and immediately pounced on by a large number of small-fry police. I ignored their demands, and asked to be taken to the chief. A Frenchman stepped up and asked me – just like that – if I would like to have lunch with him? Then the Swiss in their flash Citroen came tearing up to the cross-roads, and to the consternation of the chattering police, ripped off down another road at right angles. Mike followed in his car. I accepted the luncheon invitation, but said I had friends I must talk to first. The friends were promptly invited, in absentia. Ten minutes later Arthur drove back and said he was having a beer, and why didn't we join him? The police chief arrived, and on the Frenchman's advice, we left our passports with him and then drove to a beautiful house where the others were sitting under a spectacular wooden gazebo, a table loaded with beer in front of them. Under a thick cane roof, in a garden full of flowers of all colours, cool in the heat of the day, semi-naked in shorts and dirty from road-dust, we sat and drank with M. Rene Fijalkowski, a land surveyor, and Danielle, his wife. Lunch was agreed over drinks with the first Frenchman I had met, Nobert Roger, and later we accepted a dinner invitation from Rene and Danielle.

It was a marvellous day. Nobert was a teacher, along with his brother Alain. We went to their school and sat at a long table with a dashing-looking mechanic called Sebastian, his face scarred by four leopard claw-marks. There were other white teachers there, with names like Jacques and Jean. After soup and spaghetti, our normal road fare, we sat down to a steward-served meal of steak and salad and wine, which was incredible. We stuffed it into us, instructing our mouths in true Joycean fashion, until we were full.

Afterwards, Nobert took us swimming until 5 o'clock, when we went over to Sebastian's house to watch the daily rising of a family of hippopotamus at the bottom of his garden. And that night, in good clean clothes, drinking scotch, eating fresh Capitan fish, pizza pie, rare red steaks and sauce, it is impossible to describe without salivating. Danielle was a chef of genius. Course followed course followed course for three hours, and we had the terrible job of refusing more food. Arthur had his hair cut by Danielle, while we sat and stifled our belches. Hans ate too much and was sick. Sleeping at Sebastian's house, where the hippos promenade every morning at 3am, was no trouble at all. And this morning we were creaking wrecks of men, loath to leave, pouring coffee into our bloated stomachs and trying desperately to think what petrol and food we should order to get us to Bangui.

The French had protected us from the small-fry in the town of Bossangoa itself, but the small fry were waiting for us just outside. At 8.30am I arrived at the barrier. Half an hour later, shaking with rage, and demanding to know the name of the senior man, I was re-packing the car. The chief would not give his name. They are afraid of that, then. At last there was something we could do to stop them mauling around our cars whenever they felt like it. Threaten a letter to the premier, stating names, and however reluctantly, they would back off. Otherwise they enjoyed poking this and that, saying it was for our own protection, and claiming that we might be mercenaries. But they did not mean that. It was just idle curiosity, boredom, plus decades of resentment of white people.

The rest of the day is difficult to remember. Driving 200 miles in an Austin 7 with three pistons working over trail like a giant washboard was not invigorating. It rained, I remember, quickly, a small thunderstorm, with terrifying lightning. We passed a tree which had been struck just a few minutes before we arrived, lying across the road, shattered, like us. I must sleep. Gentle snores from the rest in this room at the Evangelist mission where we are staying.

January 15th, static in Bangui

I begin to understand the lines now, "the winter of our discontent". We are beset on all sides with troubles. The CAR has cut diplomatic relations with the Congo. There are no official ferries going across the River Ubangui. We can see the Congo on the other side. It is darker than on this side, as we imagined it must be. But some of us won't even speculate about going there. Hans has jaundice. That means he has to be flown home. After paying the fare, the two remaining Swiss, Arthur and Werner, said they would not have enough money to continue. In fact, to pay their way home, they have to sell a lot of their equipment, drive like the clappers, avoid hitch-hikers, and perhaps they will get to Zurich with enough clothes to keep out the cold, but little else.

That leaves me in a difficult situation. I have been grub-staked here. Waiting for money in Kano was too frustrating. I asked for it to be forwarded to Barclays Bank in Kampala. Werner, our treasurer, has been keeping accounts. I have saved one $10 traveller's cheque. Tomorrow I must see the American consul here, as the British consul is a Frenchman who speaks no English, and tell him about my problems. The American, Mr Burke, was pessimistic about our chances of getting into the Congo, but said he honestly had no information which was not four months out of date. This was before we knew of Hans' condition.

There has been a lot of yin and yang. We have eaten and muttered and brooded. I have done a lot of the last. The air has been thick with our languages, English, German and the vernacular. One gem has emerged. Mike, the huge German, is impatient to enter the Congo. He is full of black humour, which in our situation strikes us as terribly funny. But, he insists, it is a paradise in the Congo, and that is why we cannot get in. It is certainly going to be cheaper than here, with jam at 16/- (80p) a jar.

"We have other choices," said Vera. "Why do you want to go through the Congo?"

"Because it is ze normal way to drive to South Africa," said
Mike, earnestly.

And we have come to a temporary decision, the Swiss and
I. While I brooded in Alexa, smoking cigarette after
cigarette, Werner slowly worked out a way to Kampala. It
depends on what the American consul says tomorrow. I will
ask him to telegraph Kano, Nigeria, to see if the money I
asked for has arrived there. If it has, and in three weeks it
should have, then when we reach Kampala it should have
been forwarded on to there. That means we can go on, me in
a poorly Alexa, Arthur and Werner in the surviving Citroen.
We will either send Hans home tomorrow, or leave him with
enough money for his fare and living expenses while the
brilliant, efficient natives here take their time over arranging
his ticket.

If the money has not arrived, the surviving Swiss will
drive back to Zurich, and I will be left to my own devices. It
was as stark as that, and could be bloody.

Bangui is a city I can imagine full of mercenaries. The
French here are *chic*, and around the central square we can
sit out at café tables and watch the world go by, as in Paris.
Beggars bother us, selling, chanting, deliberately pathetic.
We have no money to spend, except Ursula, so we ignore
them. An African was knocked down by a diplomatic corps
car this morning. That was interesting. He wasn't hurt. But
the uproar drew a lot of spectators, and he acted the
wounded innocent. And the policeman, as he sauntered out
of the Palace Hotel, how important he looked, exceedingly
aware of his brief glorious moment of power.

The shadow of the Congo is over us all. It is the dominant
subject of conversation. We speculate, weighing this rumour
or that, sure of nothing. For me, it is easy. With enough
money, I will go on and perhaps through the Congo. I have
to get to Johannesburg, and with Alexa if it is humanly
possible. The others are taking their time over their
decisions. Mike bets me that Brunehilde, my typewriter, will
be acquired by the first drunken Congolese guards we meet.
I have taken his bet. We use the name Brunehilde on each

form when asked in every country for the name of my mother. In the CAR, Mike's mother was entered as Brunehilda, while his father was called Alexa. In the Congo, I will adopt those two names for my parents. Hans has regularly put as his home address the number of a certain tree in a certain street in Zurich where the prostitutes gather. There is obviously scope for imagination in the countries ahead.

But the Congo, *the Congo*, I am impatient to know what it is like. Of course there will be trouble, but how much? The atrocity stories we hear are just too much. They cannot be taken seriously. One bad incident is surely magnified, and split, until it is a hundred incidents. The American consul seemed quite relieved when I said that, if I entered the Congo, I would send him information from Kampala, if I arrive. But then, he has not seen Alexa yet, and nor will he either.

January 15/20, static, Bangui

In all we spent a week in Bangui, the second most expensive capital in the world after Washington DC, in a pipsqueak country like the CAR. Generally, our morale was bad, there were so many rumours to put us off going anywhere. Once the Swiss and Mike and I cashed in on a rumour to play a joke on Derek, Vera and Ursula.

Arthur had a small transmitter with a range of a quarter of a mile which he used to communicate with the second Citroen ID19 before it was burned. Mike was tuning in his large radio one hot damp evening, when Werner had the idea that we should trick the others into thinking that war had been declared between the CAR and the Congo. I roughed up a few passages to read, and practised my "BBC voice" once or twice, while Arthur and Mike arranged frequencies and synchronised their watches. Then Mike went into another room in the evangelist mission with his radio and began turning through the frequencies, with Derek listening idly. At the appointed time I broadcast my warning that all

Europeans should leave the Central African Republic immediately, as it was feared there would be a massacre similar to the one in the Congo in 1964.

Arthur had to hide himself he was laughing so much.

About five minutes later Vera came in white-faced and resigned, and told us our choices had gone, and all about the "war" announcement. We pretended not to believe her, but she insisted, and went off to find the missionary and tell him to flee. I thought the joke should go on for perhaps half an hour, us continuing to scoff, Derek and Vera and Ursula continuing to speculate darkly on our fate. Mike hugged his radio and was very happy with the joke, which he wanted to continue for a week. Arthur and Werner looked happy for the first time in days. In the end, of course, the joke was revealed and it was taken very well.

It was one of the few bright spots in that week of gloom.

To convince Werner, in particular, about the real existence of my money, I phoned Mr McManus, my editor on the *Irish Independent* in Dublin, to ask if it had been forwarded. It cost my last $10 traveller's cheque, and took three hours for a rotten connection to be made. I was relieved to find my articles were being published, and discovered money had been sent to my agent in London, Hope Leresche, with instructions to forward it. When I told this to Werner and Arthur, they were still not satisfied that the money would be in Kampala to re-pay their grubstake, and were almost settled on driving back to Zurich.

On January 17, Hans flew home, nursing his jaundice, via Paris, with my articles to post and a short letter to Fiona....

...I cannot pull punches. It is a difficult situation. Not impossible, though. We can get visas for the Congo. I plan to go from Bangui to Lisala, up by riverboat to Kisangani (Stanleyville), join a military convoy to Beni and out from there. In Uganda in two weeks, I hope. Seven of us going through. We leave on the 21st. Leave any messages at American Express in Kampala. How many times each day I think of you. At nights you dominate the sky. I lie on my back and look at you. Not long now.

There is little else I can say that I have not said in the articles. My morale is good. It falters sometimes, but I think of you and that's it. The Swiss need moral support, chivvying, but they are finally coming. What is it going to be like in the Congo? No one really knows. We listen to rumour after rumour. Kampala is our goal now. We say the word often...

Hans also took a letter which he posted first class from Paris to my agent, Mrs Leresche, asking her to phone me on Monday, January 20, at the US Embassy. It was marvellous when she did so, and told me she had personally sent £100 to Kampala, and had heard that Mr McManus had sent an additional £50 there too. That was easily enough money to cover my grubstake. At this news the Swiss were satisfied.

Visas for the Congo were a song-and-dance act. They cost £2.10.0 each, were valid for a month, and I am certain some pockets were lined. Derek arranged a ferry for us to travel across the Ubangui River, by some means which he never revealed. The ferryboat had been a gift from the Congo to the CAR, and in the strained atmosphere, it had not been used for months, so all the more credit to Derek for getting us transport across...

CHAPTER 13
The Congo

At the time the AA Guide was published, the country later known as Zaire was known as Congo – Leopoldville (now known again as the Congo). Since the guide appeared in 1960, the Congo had acquired a dreadful reputation for massacres of white people, former Belgian colonists. It was a huge country with a population of 15 million, and its capital Leopoldville was later renamed Kinshasa. The climate was tropical, except for the western coastal districts, with very high temperatures and rain. There had been an extensive road system which was deteriorating, nearly all of it all-weather, mostly gravel but some tarmac in Katanga, the copper and cobalt-rich province which attempted to break away to become independent. Heavy rains were expected in February, a couple of weeks after our arrival.

The guide to the roads, from Bangui via Banzyville and Yakoma to the Congo River, said they were untarred, but heavy rain may hold up the traffic for short periods. There was said to be petrol on route, but this didn't exist, except at the extensive mission centres all over the country.

January 21 - February 9, 1969. 36,454 - 37,619 (1,165 miles) 5,234 - 7,399 miles from London

January 21, Zongo Mission

We're in, at last. The shenanigans today finally resulted in a boat trip across the Ubangui River, but the delay left us all irritable. This evening it is difficult to say a civil word to one another, though no one remarks on it. There are eight cars inside the grounds of this mission in Zongo, all travelling the same route, all "tourists". Twenty one people. Our Grauenhalft Safari has an addition, a German Volkswagen with three Berliners, 24 days out of Berlin, in a hurry to see the parks in Kenya. Arthur and Werner were in two minds, right to the end, about whether to attempt the Congo, but decided to do so after a nerve-racking series of doubts. Derek Haldane has his Landrover here, and Mike, the huge German with his Citroen 2CV, he at least has no doubts which route he will take, and is satisfied to be in the Congo.

The other three cars are Landrovers. Two are driven quickly by free-spending Italian doctors, who have a remarkable knack for getting things done in central Africa. The third has four British people in it, George and Margaret, Bill and Barbara. I expect that, once through the self-important customs check tomorrow, they will belt on ahead of us to Lisala, arriving there tomorrow night if they have luck. Perhaps they will take a riverboat to Kisangani, as we plan to do, and drive up good track to Kampala. But if the boat takes longer than a day to arrange, the Italians are in favour of driving through Buta and east to Isiro (Paulis), along the route I had originally planned before I heard there was trouble with Sudanese refugees in that region.

Today we went through all the formalities for leaving the CAR before 9 o'clock in the morning. Our cars were filled with petrol, carnets were stamped out, exit-stamps in our passports, pink cards filled in for the ferry, food bought. We lined the cars down a ramp waiting for the Congolese consul to come with us as protection against a feared attack on the ferry pilot. All day we waited as Frenchmen scuttled down to inform us of the latest rumour. There were said to be field guns lined up on the opposite bank ready to fire on us. Bokassa, president of the CAR, with an army of 500 men, was playing heroic games, threatening Mobutu, president of the Congo, with an army of 40,000 men. Everyone was waiting for Mobutu's reply to Bokassa's challenge – "If Mobutu wants war, he shall have it!" How much of this is true, no one really knows. We had to live with the rumours. They were effective in frightening us.

It was the consensus of opinion that those of us planning to go across the river were being used as pawns to decide which way Bokassa or Mobutu would jump. If we got to the other side and were arrested or shot, or the ferry was impounded, then Bokassa would know exactly how angry Mobutu was. If, on the other hand, the ferry was allowed to return to the CAR, then Mobutu was not really that angry, and Bokassa could play it from there. For seven hours we stewed with that knowledge, each whim of Bokassa carried by eager rumour to us to gauge our reaction. Finally, at 4 o'clock, the Congolese consul arrived – without his luggage, so he was not doing a bunk – and we set off.

The ferry pilot was so terrified he steered straight into the opposite bank, and damaged a pontoon jetty, but we were able to drive off before sundown.

The delays left us irritated. We could only take it out on each other. There were tired moans at dinner tonight, petty bickering, injured dignities, and these may become normal for the whole drive through the Congo. The frequent road blocks we have been told to expect will not improve matters, and nor will the difficulty we will have in deciding the route from the two or three possible routes to get to Lisala. The last matter seems settled now. Tomorrow is another day.

At least the Swiss cannot threaten to go home. They must go on to Uganda. Even today, they said that if the ferry did not cross before nightfall, they would return to Switzerland tomorrow. Writing it down now, looking at it in print, the whole matter seems petty. We have narrow horizons at the moment. I admit to being blind to any other matter than getting to Kampala through the Congo. No other route is possible for me.

Alexa went well, all of 4 miles today. Yesterday Arthur and I replaced the smashed front spring and tightened the shock absorbers. It makes a terrific difference. No more wallowing over the road, crashing the axle on to the spring mounting. The car has to be pushed up steep ramps now. I feel that a day's run will leave a layer of coke around the pistons and increase engine compression. It will need it. The mountains rise to over 9,000 feet in the east.

My hands are ripped to shreds. Areas of skin, layers deep, perhaps half an inch square, have been torn off by the loose ferrule on the starting handle. When the engine is warm and I have had to stop it, starting requires 20 or 25 energetic heaves on the handle. On the boat up to Kisangani, Arthur says he will mend the starting motor. Meanwhile, we persevere.

At Kampala, hopefully two weeks and a thousand frightened rumours away, I pick up money for the last stage of the journey. I am looking forward to it. Some will be spent on a party, tearing the slats off a few bars there. Some will be paid back to Arthur and Werner for grub-staking me here. The rest will give me a blessed freedom again.

January 22/23 (written on January 24) driven 312 miles to Kota-Koli

The Italian catholic fathers at the Zongo mission, across the river from Bangui, were marvellous. They doled out beer, sat us down, told us the route we should take — east to Banzyville and Yakoma, across three ferries to Buta — and then played a practical joke which gave them great amusement. The English girl who found the monkey in her tent took it very well, even though the monkey had pee'd there before being discovered. Later in the night I talked to a Belgian engineer, a M. Paen. He had put up the lamps in the jungle which the people in Bangui thought were preparations for an invasion. M.Paen also told me that the vaunted army of 40,000 fearsome Congolese that was scaring the daylights out of the CAR actually numbers 31 men.

I was first to go through customs and passport control the next day. The others wanted to make as much mileage as possible. I have the slowest car, need it be said? A fat Buddha-like officer hustled me through, fingering my papers gingerly, ordering his men to make only a quick search of my car. He was interested in making money from us, certainly, but I looked a very poor prospect. But he was going to check everything, because we were the first "tourists" over the river in months. What had happened to Roger Phelps, the Englishman in the Thames van whom the Swiss had seen off from Nigeria? We made enquiries, but no news. I could not wait to ask more questions, and by 9.15am, having been held up for only two hours, I left Zongo.

Despite previous plans, we all agreed to follow the south bank of the Ubangui River to get to Buta, which is not supposed to be a trouble spot now, according to M.Paen, though it had been recently. I drove to Boyabo and turned left, and 40 miles out of Zongo, I was joined by the three Berliners in a Volkswagon. They stayed for a while, but later in the day I had to clean Alexa's oil jets, and they pushed on. I have since heard they are 200 kms ahead of me. We expected them to leave us as soon as the river was crossed.

Mike in his Citroen 2CV came up just as they were leaving, and for the rest of the day, he and I drove together. I had one puncture. As it grew dark, we were covering the last few miles to the Catholic mission at Bossobolo. He drove ahead with his lights on, while I followed, trying to judge the terrain by what I could see behind his tail lights. It will be a relief to have my headlights back in Kampala.

There were Italian fathers again at the mission, a huge place, but only two of them. I was very tired. In French, our only common language – and I seem to be getting worse at it, not better – we tried to ask about the route ahead, and exchanged pleasantries over dinner. Where were the others?

The fast Italian Landrovers, Derek and Vera, and the Swiss? No sign of them. That fat man must have held them there until he was bribed. The tourist business is not good here, and pickings are lean.

I went to bed at 8.30, so tired I did not hear the others arrive. They were all there in the morning. Some of us had breakfast at the mission, lovely coffee, bread and jam, and again I was first away. Looking at my map, I thought I might get to Yakoma by evening, but my estimates were more often wrong than right these days. After a puncture at lunchtime, I passed through Banzyville at 2pm, past hundreds of parading children under a sign saying "Soyez le Bienvenus" (Welcome). A group of policemen in dark glasses shot past me in a Landrover going the other way. I could see they were startled at Alexa, and did not know whether to stop or not. Out of the other side of town I watched my rear-view mirror, but when I waved gaily out of the window, it seemed to calm their doubts.

The Italians had passed me in the morning, stopping to take hundreds of photographs while I gave them a message for the Austin agents in Kampala. I thought Austin might be interested when I got through the Congo. George, the English chap with three others in a Landrover, was with them. Later I saw Derek's distinctive Landrover in my rear-view mirror. He stayed with me for about half an hour; I have not seen him since. I know Arthur had to fix suspension trouble with his Citroen driving into Bossobolo. Perhaps he has got more trouble now?

The countryside is beautiful here. Rich, thick vegetation, with views over rolling valleys from the tops of hills, the constant wide river. All the villagers seem friendly. We were told to avoid villages; people around here are supposed to hate whites. But Mobutu has brought the Belgians back, one by one, to help put the Congo straight, so perhaps it is not so bad now.

The roads are very bad. No washboard, but a lot of sand and very deep pot-holes. Sometimes the car literally fell down hills. About an hour and a half out of Banzyville, I drove over a solid lump of mud, there was a terrific bang and my brakes ceased to work. On top of that, I had another puncture. I mended the puncture on the road, keeping an eye cocked for the others. They did not appear. My spare tyre, an old bald remould, still has not been mended after a slow puncture on the first night into the Congo. I was rather sad when it went down for the first time. All the other tyres were more good-looking, and had punctured at least once, and I was proud that the bald one had held out for so long.

The brakes were another business. I could not camp by the side of the road. There was a mission at Kota-Koli, 30 miles away. I had an hour and a half to make it there before darkness. Three black men stopped to talk to me as I was topping up the petrol tank, and told me the mission was on top of a high cliff, after a lot of sand. I drove on.

The sand was bad, particularly with reduced power on 3 pistons. Each time I stuck, however, villagers appeared. I asked them to push me out, and on doing so, each got a cigarette. In this way I made it to the bottom of the winding road up the cliff before sundown. But there was not enough power in the engine to take me to the top and I stuck halfway, unable to get over the last hump, even with three villagers pushing, and, brakeless, in constant danger of rolling backwards and wrecking the car.

I left the car in gear, turned the engine off and, with natives straining to hold her, blocked the back wheels with large stones. In exchange for one frying-pan, which was cluttering up the car anyway, a native went to the mission with a note asking for help. As the sun was setting, over the top of the hill came a jeep full of missionaries, their white cassocks flying in the wind, followed by a Landrover with two smart Belgian commando captains. They were all white. Aware of a certain style about the situation, I went into a Stanley and Livingstone act, which was greeted with beams and smiles. A Brother Florentine towed me to the mission before it became too dark to see anything, but he forgot I had no brakes. When he stepped on his brakes, I stopped on him.

In the mission, a beautiful large white building looking

over distant green hills, one of the Belgian commandos – Captain Sonkt – was celebrating his sixth wedding anniversary with his wife. In my dusty jean shorts, filthy with dust but excited to have arrived, I took a beer and joined in the toast to their health. The other Belgian officer, Captain Gaston Bebronne, commanding officer of a Congolese army training camp of 500 soldiers nearby, asked me how I had got here. The four missionaries, Fathers Joseph, Ludolf and John, plus Brother Florentine seemed delighted to have me, and handed around champagne. Afterwards, we ate.

I was given a room next to the main terrace.

This morning I found when I looked at Alexa that the timing case is broken, having struck the back to the jeep the previous night. Oil was leaking out on to the ground, though the radiator seemed fine. I have no money, not a penny. Arthur and Werner and Derek and Mike have not arrived. If they heard in Molegbwe, the village before Banzyville, that the ferry boat in Yakoma isn't working, as I have now heard, perhaps they turned south to Businga. Somehow I feel detached from the problem. Alexa will have to be fixed, and I must go on.

Captain Bebronne has told me he did his initial commando training in Britain. He speaks English slowly but well. He took me along to meet his soldiers this morning. They are the finest black soldiers I have seen, very cool, sure of themselves. The captain told them about my car, and afterwards he bought me 500 cigarettes because I told him I had none, and then showed me his camp, driving me around in a jeep until we came to four deep holes in the ground.

"Do you know what they are for?" he asked, and when I said I didn't, he told me that if he caught his men asleep on duty, and wanted to punish them, he buried them alive up to their necks in the holes for 24 hours. He was an extraordinary man. His whole authority seemed to rest on his personality, and he and Captain Sonkt had impressed themselves on their troops in the same way a Red Indian Chief, or the leader of a Scottish clan, did 200 years ago.

Captain Bebronne said he would have Alexa fixed for me. I drove her into his camp where a bunch of Congolese mechanics fell on her, taking her to pieces. How many days will it take? Where are Arthur and Derek and the others? I am flat broke.

"Of course you must stay here as long as you like," said Father Rudolf. He spent 25 years in India, and speaks English well. But where to from here?

(The others arrived three hours after I had finished writing this account. Mike, despite taking anti-malaria tablets daily, promptly went down with malaria. He was joined by Werner, Derek and Vera. Arthur and I were untouched, although I took no precautions at all. We decided to stay at Kota-Koli for a while until the others recovered, and Alexa was mended. I became a minor celebrity.)

January 25/26, 1969. Molegbwe and the consecration of a Congolese bishop

Captain Bebronne looks like the comic strip character, Battler Britton, all jaw and steely eye. He likes reading TE Lawrence and also Oscar Wilde. He is not terribly fond of Arthur, who looks like a gypsy, while he took a shine to me, hair bleached by the sun, fair complexion, blue eyes. He has pointedly invited me, alone, as his guest at a ceremony to consecrate a Congolese Bishop. I took notes…

"Woke at 4am, shaved, dressed in 3-piece suit, ready by 5am, jeep took me to Capt Sonkt's house, coffee. He and his wife make loving jokes, even over breakfast. Drove to Banzyville through morning mist, killing one chicken. We picked up a letter and refused lifts to everyone. I was interested in the road, having driven Alexa over it to Kota-Koli.

"Lovely breakfast; ham, salami and more coffee. Then we belted along more crowded roads to Molegbwe. Now, 8.20, Capt Sonkt is washing, changing into Number One's. The sun has broken through. A pretty girl in a single shift brings water to wash our hands.

"'Who does she belong to?' asked the captain. His men grin at each other and joke, polishing their shoes. Everyone's going to Molegbwe.

"Very social occasion. Captain Sonkt and I shake hands with everyone else. Bebronne is already here, just two white army officers in a sea of black soldiers. The brothers and fathers of all the missions we stayed at are here. One is smoking a cigarette behind his cupped hand. Tut! I have just seen a general. He has sunglasses, of course. He looks very serious."

The consecration took place on a football field, with trees all around it, like beech trees at home, but they were full of people. A long thatched shelter was built along one of the sidelines, obviously a grandstand. Officers and dignitaries sat there, plus one black hunchback with a strong face full of character and his trousers pulled by braces up his twisted body to his chest. A small thatched shelter faced the grandstand, where the centre circle cut the halfway line. Fathers and brothers sat on chairs around three sides of the small shelter, leaving the grandstand a good view. There were five photographers. Three chewed gum constantly throughout the proceedings in true American newsreel fashion. They moved everywhere, absorbed in their art and their appearance as artists.

Behind the father and brothers were little boys, lined four deep, sitting in grey shorts and shirts, prepared to sing when ordered, as they were occasionally. Then, protecting the square, Captain Bebronne's commandos, smart and self-contained. I stood with the crowd that managed to shuffle just in front of the troops. Behind me were open spaces, then an extremely large crowd that, halfway through the morning, was let loose to push and shove for a better view.

"Waiting, moving restlessly. Air smells sweaty. Old sweat. A baby wails, tries to suck at its mother's breast, mother holds it to her dress. Girls in bright costumes enter arena, bowls of fruit on their heads. Procession follows, Catholic, like home – waft of incense, chant of Latin.

"*The bishop-designate looks young, about 35. African music now, off-beat bongo drums. More wailing babies, whistles blow, crowd pushes, then....quiet. A white priest reads in sonorous Latin. Cameras everywhere. It's 9.30 and getting hot (18,000 bottles of cold beer, and 120 bottles of scotch whisky have been laid on for the feast afterwards, Captain Bebronne said).*

"*Trees shake and crack with people. Priests and brothers, in white cassocks, bearded like old poets, rose and fell in their seats as the speakers come and go. Two vultures circle overhead. Terribly long message from the Pope, read in French and native dialect, by a black priest who milks every word. I walk away, sweaty, wanting a smoke.*

"*A little boy smiles and holds out his hand. 'Me donnez cadeau' he says, give me a present. His mother laughs. One day soon I'll die, I think. It must have been the occasion. I give him nothing, for I have nothing to give.*

"*Back in the crowd at 10.30. More babies cry. The ceremony is over. Clapping, wailing, cheers like singing. Girls with fruit approach the new bishop. The captains are bare-headed; it must be hot under a beret. In the crowd a woman pulls at her dress, gives her breast to her baby. Nearby, six crones cackle and grimace.*

"*11am. The vultures may be ungainly on the ground, hobbling with a one-two cadence, like a man with one rubber leg, but they are beautiful in the air. Two of them soar like gliders, thermal climbing in a hot bubble broken from the slate roofs of the football changing rooms behind the grandstand. Then, in a long gentle glide, balancing on air, they slide away towards the trees. Two more join them. They have found another thermal. Lazy Saturday morning.*

"*I wonder how many here are really Christians?*

"*12.30, lunch, after a slow march by all the dignitaries (plus me) back to the primary school. Social hoo-haas when I could produce no invitation. Captain Bebronne being very mess-military. 'I don't know who's the chief of protocol here,' he said. I sit myself with Christian humbleness at the bottom of the table and thankfully drink a beer. It isn't cold. I wonder if I can smoke without a celestial thunderbolt wiping me out?*

"*Bishop arrives, like a successful politician, arms crucified over both lines of tables between which he walks. We stand, they clap.*

"Drinking here is like drinking alone.

"1.45, ceased to be humble, moved to near top of the table at Captain Sonkt's invitation. Drinking boiler-makers, beer with whisky chasers, and talking too much. There will be seven speeches..."

At this point my writing started to slope towards the bottom right hand corner of my notebook, and I became muddled. Once, after being told boilermakers were lethal, I brought Captain Bebronne over to argue my case for me, that I could take them. Later, I remember challenging one of the brothers, who had a sad face with a long black beard and indrawn eyes, and asking him about his Christian faith. I suddenly realised halfway through his slow stammering answer that he had lost all but the shell of his faith, after the murderous last 10 years in the Congo, and my brash shallowness was hurtful to him. I felt ashamed to even appear to have some answers on God, that He didn't exist and we had to make our own way in life.

"4.10. Right down inside myself, sitting behind the saluting platform waiting for the commandos to march past, I realise I am getting jingled. Drunk is a better, more vulgar word. It is not funny. I am white. It is interesting to see my writing is getting more childish.

"4.30. I have told Captain Bebronne that he is responsible for me, that he should warn me sternly when I am being foolish. Captain Sonkt has gone back to his wife. This should be an interesting night. A commando is telling a group of people about my 'exploits'. Phoo."

In this state of mind, then, I celebrated with 2,000 others the consecration of a Congolese bishop. But in a black man's country I needed something familiar, and with all the other white men, Captain Bebronne and I ended up in a Belgian doctor's house in Banzyville, about 60kms from Molegbwe. We ate there, and talked, and I came to realise I was drinking for England.

It became a point of national honour some time in the
night to sink every drink offered, and remain standing. By a
miracle, for I do not have a strong head, I succeeded, even to
talking coherently. A poor young Belgian called Jules failed,
and was rude to everyone in a very excited way. Captain
Bebronne verbally tore him to pieces and Jules slunk away
into the night. Two moments remain for me. One was a
question, "do you understand the poem at the beginning of
Seven Pillars of Wisdom?" asked the captain. I knew it was
widely regarded as a love poem from TE Lawrence to a
young Arab boy, so I was guarded in my reply. Bebronne
shook his head slowly, as if the question had always bothered
him. And later, "you're lucky," he said, "for you have your
situation." He struck me as a man without a situation, much
like Napoleon would have been had he been born 30 years
earlier and had been middle-aged at the time of the French
Revolution. It was 2am when the party broke up. We slept at
the doctor's house.

On Sunday, I had the mother of all hangovers, while
Bebronne took me around all the Belgian houses. I managed,
by turning off any coherent thought, to stay on my feet until
11 o'clock, but the first sight of a beer was too much, and I
was sick as a dog every fifteen minutes for the next two
hours. We all suffered after consecrating that bishop.

I learned one more thing, that a white man seems to have
his choice of most black girls in the Congo. Bebronne was
driving me through a village when he stopped to talk to a
very pretty black girl. I could not understand what they
were saying, but his easy attitude and her smiling flirtatious
replies made me think she was his mistress. After we drove
off I asked him if that was the case.

"Absolutely not," he replied. "I can't let my men know their
captain fucks".

Did he know the girl? No, it was the first time he had
talked to her. Why did he not want his soldiers to
know?....but I could not ask that question. He had his own
special God he lived with, and his own answers for the way
he lived.

Lunch, and we slept until 4pm, then the captain's jeep arrived and we tore back to the mission. I felt, as I walked up the stairs and greeted Derek and Ursula, a shadow of the man who had left the day before. It was difficult trying to gather the impressions to tell the others. They must have felt I had been slacking, and holding them up. I suppose I had been.

At dinner that night, at 7 o'clock as usual, I was aware I would have to work hard on Alexa to prepare her for leaving. On the wall of the dining room, next to the black-bordered picture of a brother who was murdered by Simbas five years earlier, outside in the mission square, an empty frame hung waiting for a suitable photograph of the new bishop. I rather liked that empty frame. It gave an extra dimension to the room, but it stayed empty until we left, four days later.

January 29, 1969 - Mission Kota-Koli

I have been here now for six days, the others for five. They arrived a few hours after I wrote my last journal, when I was wondering what to do about the snapped brake cables and the smashed timing case. We have remained here since for a number of reasons. First, malaria has put many of us down. Second, Captain Bebronne, to his great embarrassment, could not come through on promises to weld the timing case together, and we have been considering how to solve that problem. Third, the area is so short of mechanics that Arthur and Derek are in full demand, fixing everything from a huge air-strip scraper to small, cheap radios.

Bar the bishop's beer bash, I spent each day working on Alexa. Congolese mechanics stripped it down in short order, but putting it back together again was another story. The timing case also held the starting handle, and had a recess cut to take the pulley which revolved at the end of the cam-shaft, serving by fan-belt the water-pump and fan. At first, when we heard the case could not be welded together – it was aluminium – we spent two days wondering if a wooden case would serve. Yes, said Bebronne, he could get us some

ebony, we could shape it correctly and bolt it on to the front
of the crank-case, discarding the starting handle. But the
pulley bothered us, and after some debate we decided to glue
the case back together, cut out the starting handle, shorten
the long shank which contained the handle, and then glue a
piece of tin can across the gap to keep the oil in.

It sounded desperate, and of course, it was. But I believed
it might work. We push-started the engine again and there
was no oil leakage. We looked at the starter-motor, which
appears perfect, but we could not get it to work. Naturally,
without a starting handle, or a motor, we were reduced to
pushing the car to start it from now on. I could see a few
problems ahead when I was cut off from the others and my
engine died halfway up a hill, but resolved to solve those
when they occurred.

As for the brakes, they do not work too well. The lump of
hard mud which snapped the cables also snapped the spring
which took the brakes off when I lifted my foot off the pedal.
I decided I would drive without brakes most times, saving
them for emergencies, and control my speed through gear
changes. Every time I put the brakes on and the emergency
was over, I had to get out of the car and physically pull the
brake levers off on each wheel. We would see how it worked.
As far as the brakes and timing case were concerned, the
methods I was forced to use were the last choices. At
Kampala, everything could be corrected, but Kampala was a
long way away.

The others had been impatient immediately after their
arrival, when they heard about the broken timing case. But
the missionaries ran an open house, beds, food, beer in the
cool evening, a fine view over rich green hills from the long
terrace, and they all decided to stay until Alexa was fixed. It
turned out to be a prudent decision. On January 24, when the
first group arrived, Werner went down with malaria. He was
in bed for three days, being dosed with quinine. Ursula was
also ill, but we could not diagnose her malady. In her typical
off-hand fashion, forgetting one minute what she had said
five minutes earlier, she thought she had everything from

jaundice to death-watch beetle. Next day Mike, the German teacher, who had handed out a hundred admonitions to me about my carelessness with water, who was always so careful himself with his mosquito nets and cream and dutifully-taken tablets, well, the book failed Mike and he took to his bed with the worst case of malaria I had seen. He was out until yesterday. Today he felt well enough to drive. Derek and Vera, the two Scots, now felt ill, and Arthur and I, fit as fleas throughout the trip, talked apprehensively to each other, wondering when it was going to be our turn *(In my case it was three months later, in South Africa, when I reached a temperature of 106 F)*. My problem of course, was a relief driver.

Meanwhile we worked each day and talked each night. Arthur chaffed and stamped around with nothing to do, until he was told that the giant earth-scraper which was meant to be used to lay out an air-strip a mile up the road, had not worked since it arrived. The Congolese had laid a thousand yards by sheer physical effort, shovel and bucket. Arthur gave a whoop and was away the next day, hotly pursued by Derek, to fix the thing.

What an impression they made! Received as minor gods, surrounded by Africans, covered in dirt and oil, happy as sand-boys, speaking German, English and a fractured French, the two of them fixed the machine and took over the camp. One bulldozer for Derek to minister to next day, a lorry for Arthur, watches, radios, a tape-recorder were showered on them, all needing mending. We thought yesterday it might be difficult to get away. Captain Bebronne got a glint in his eye that indicated he might be thinking of holding on to us. His Africans could not believe it when we said we had to leave. But why, they asked us, over and over again. Don't you like it here? Arthur and Derek were offered jobs at £250 a month, a free house each, water, electricity, servants. We declined as gently as we could.

Two nights ago we had dinner at Captain Sonkt's house. They lived in a bungalow he built himself near the mission. Labour was no problem. He said he just stopped passers-by

and said, "you're working for me, and you, and you", and it
was completed in 6 weeks. Mike was still in bed, but the rest
of us went, with Father Ludorf. Vera cut my hair to make me
presentable. It was a lovely dinner, excellent spaghetti,
unlimited drink - scotch, brandy, beer for me. We all drank
and talked a lot. Bebronne really came out of his shell and
told us about his life, and more particularly, his ambitions.

I had already said he worshipped Lawrence of Arabia.
Arthur, a blunt talker at the best of times, had outraged
Bebronne by referring to the roads in the Congo in very
sarcastic terms. That night, largely because of Arthur's
repair work, their differences were made up. But I knew
Bebronne was prejudiced against Arthur, because with his
brown face and dark moustache, Arthur looked like a gypsy,
and Bebronne had this thing about blond supermen. There
was one delicate and terrifying moment, just past midnight.
Father Ludolf had just gone to sleep, and the rest of us were
thinking of leaving. Bebronne had, by this time, consumed
more than a bottle of scotch, and his voice was slow and
deliberate.

"What will you do with your car if you cannot get it
through?" he asked me.

"I'll burn it."

"If you do, I promise you I will kill you. Nothing should be
burned in the Congo. The Congo needs everything. If the
car doesn't go, I will give you a house, food, everything, and
get you to the British ambassador as soon as possible. He's a
friend of mine ("but he'll send me back to England", I
thought frantically, "and I'll have to set out again for South
Africa to marry"). I forbid you to burn the car. I promise you,
I'll find you and kill you if you do."

The others didn't say anything, and neither did I. Of
course, I believed him. Who would stop him in the Congo?
We sat and were thoughtful for a while, not saying anything,
until the girls got up to leave, and we followed them. I
remain determined to burn the car if she cannot possibly
ever get through, but I resolved to keep quiet about it until
the time came. I hoped more than ever that it didn't.

We are ready to leave. Our safari has a new member, a
small monkey which Vera bought Derek as a late birthday
present. He has been wanting one for weeks. I am sorry to
say they christened it Bebronne. We dare not tell anybody
here. I hope it likes travelling. I don't think it is house-
broken, and may have to wear a nappy.

We should make Yakoma, 60 miles away, by night fall. It is
1.30 in the afternoon now. It is a relief to be moving again.
This day will tell about the car's condition.

January 29/30, 1969, Kota-Koli to Bodalangi via Yakoma, 180 miles

It is getting near the end. She cannot last much longer. I
cannot think what might happen when I have to destroy her.
How has she even survived the last 180 miles? I don't know.
I feel despondent, more so in that I cannot show it. The
others have, I feel, already given her up as a bad job. They
are waiting for her to collapse. It seems criminal, also absurd,
for me to keep telling them how rotten each day is, crashing
and stumbling over deep rain furrows, losing pieces here and
there.

If you could see the car now, or I could see her with your
eyes, perhaps I might stop. Sometimes I open my eyes and
see her for what she really is. Starting from London, brakes
working, lights ready to snap on when I turned the switch,
four pistons, nearly perfect. Now, though she still goes, she is
a wreck, dying hard. No lights; lost them in the Sahara, and
if I put in replacements the *piste* will shake them out again.
My brakes haven't worked, at all, for the past two days. I go
down hills with the engine in low gear. It can be fairly hairy.
There were one or two bad moments, such as a concealed log
bridge, the centre higher than the sides, water below, at the
bottom of a hill. I nearly went into the water, missed by
inches. Probably I would not have killed myself.
Nevertheless, I shook afterwards.

The starter still doesn't work, and the starting handle had
to be permanently removed when we glued together the

timing case. Thank God that glue works, and I am losing only a little oil. To start the car in the morning, the others push it. As I have driven ahead of them most of the time, when the engine stops I have to have patience. If it is on a hill – and it has not been yet – then I am fine, roll down, crash into second gear and we are away. Otherwise I wait five minutes until the curious natives approach, then bribe them with cigarettes to push-start the car. Today I spent 8 cigarettes, in batches of 3, 2 and 3. No one has held out for money, which is lucky, as I have none. Werner gave me the small sum of $7 to pay for petrol, should the others lose me. I will still continue to use cigarettes for push-starting.

The small apron on the front of the radiator, with the car's number on it, was bashed off today. I kept it as a souvenir. The accelerator arm, leading to the pedal, lost its rubber band, which was replaced. I have learned the knack of climbing large hills with reduced power, after that unfortunate incident at Kota-Koli. I roll down hills – they come in ups and downs, together, rarely alone – engine in second gear, shrieking away. At a moment which I cannot explain, it is a feeling – wham! – all stops out, go like the clappers over the last downhill ruts, and shriek uphill, dropping a gear each time the engine fades. It has worked, so far. If it doesn't, I will be stuck on the hill, no brakes to stop it rolling backwards, just keep the engine in gear and switch off and wait, in the hope that the reduced compression on three pistons will act as a brake. Perhaps I could keep slipping the clutch, bellowing Mayday, but the prospect of bargaining for a push while hanging on for grim death is both amusing and terrifying.

I want to save my typewriter, Brunehilde. I wonder if one of the others will take it for me? In the event of a crash, which seems inevitable, it would get really damaged.

But, I assert, nothing is inevitable.

I have not looked at a map to see how far it is to go.

Each day is valid unto itself. One day we will arrive. Yesterday I knew this would be the final trial for the car. It is either Kampala, which seems like paradise, or bust.

Captain Bebronne saw us off. There was a mix-up; he had my camera, and I set off from the mission first to get it, and somehow the others passed me. The captain set off after them, hunched over the wheel of his jeep, to tell them to wait for me. We made the mission at Yakoma after dark. I hung out of my window with a hurricane lamp so the others could see me, and drove by the lights of Mike's tail-lights and the beam of the Swiss car's spotlights behind me.

(I interrupted this narrative to kill a rat in the bathroom of the Mission Bodalangi. Derek and I drove it out with sticks. I could not bring myself to kill it, when Ursula fell upon it, delivering six great blows, counting each one. It was dead afterwards. With two sticks, I carried it outside and flung its body into the tall grass. Ursula was pretty good, an amazing woman. Mike, huge Mike, would not go near it, even when it was dead. It was terrified. Poor rat.)

January 31, Bodalangi to the Unilever Plantation east of Bumba, 55 miles

I was very irritated last night, but after Ursula killed the rat, somehow it seemed to go. The two fathers at the mission gave us breakfast this morning after their mass, and saw us off. Because the mission is 7 miles off the main route, and that main route is rarely driven by "tourists", we had been very welcome. One of the fathers had not seen a "tourist" in 19 years.

The road to Bumba was the usual shocking *piste*, a series of ups and downs, with small bridges, five or six logs buried in the ground. I have perfected the trick of getting the right wheel plumb on to a log and driving the car at a slight angle to the line of the road, so the left wheel does not fall between logs. There are times, though, when I fail. Once the car leapt off a bridge, impossible to slow down without brakes, and entered a series of troughs. After each trough we leapt higher and higher, until by the end of the fourth trough I had lost control. The car took off and plumped on to the road, swerved – the steering has been loose for ages, though the column no longer falls away from its retaining bracket – and we dived into a huge hole next to the jungle. I could not drive her out, and waited for the others to come and help.

When we pulled her out the clutch felt weak. I have been more than usually careful ever since, not telling the others. At 11.30 we hit the main route from Lisala to Bumba, and half an hour later the army post outside the town waved us down. After 15 minutes, all of us feigning ignorance of French, the army's curiosity was satisfied, and we drove into town to get petrol for Alexa. The others had enough to get to Akati.

For the first and last time we saw the Congo River, but we did not swim in it, as we had once said we would, because it was too dangerous. In the hot day, languishing by the petrol station, we were objects of great curiosity, yet not great enough to persuade the pump attendant from taking his lunchtime siesta. He said he would give us petrol at 2 o'clock, a wait of an hour and a half. Irritation, calmed by a few beers, and the antics of Derek's monkey. Derek is teaching it to drink like a gentleman, and be more circumspect in its toilet.

When we finally received petrol, the police in town caught us. Two authorities run the Congo, the army and the police, and they work against each other. If we enter a town and are checked out by the army, we then have to see the police and be checked out by them too. Captain Bebronne's name is getting us past a lot of delays. I often say he will be angry if we are held up. They ask if we truly know him, and when I say we stayed six days with him, they back off. Even though we are 250 miles away from him, his name carries great weight. But if we miss being checked out by one of the authorities, they will telegraph ahead to have us apprehended. Of course, the telegraph system here is ludicrous, and one can chance a quick drive through towns, but it keeps our nerves on edge.

Derek had heard about a Unilever plantation outside Bumba, and we thought we might try the hospitality there instead of the mission at Lolo. After some enquiries, and an amicable talk with the local police, we found that the plantation was 10 miles down a road which forked off to the left after a river bridge. I led the way in, down cool straight avenues for miles. We got lost, resolved to keep driving east, and eventually found a white man. He brought us to the director, and after some hesitation which we didn't understand then, but do now, they put us up in the maison-de-passage. We became aware that we would have to pay, but we were never actually told. This uncertainty brought other things to a head, and we fought it all out over dinner. It was pretty rough. Mike was castigated first for cracking jokes with the police, asking to take photos, not realising that his air of self-certainty and his huge size, coupled with his apparent richness, made the Congolese resent him, and all of us to some degree. Gradually we all brought out our resentments, and there was some hysteria, tears from the girls, and it was better afterwards. Mike, in his German way, thought we should sing a solidarity song. I told him that was not our way of doing things. We started to crack jokes.

February 1/2, Unilever plantation to Buta, 183 miles

I have a tatty note that I wrote that day that survived the rest of the journey. It was written at 3.40 in the afternoon, after having driven 71 miles that day....

   ...sitting by the side of the road with a broken radiator. Derek and Mike have gone on to Aketi, 40 kms away, to the catholic mission there. Werner is soldering the radiator, using my Primus as a heat source, and a screw-driver. It's a hot, sticky day, being eaten alive by flies. Stuck in sand four times, pushed out three times, pulled out once. Have removed front brake cable as one end was smashed. Carburettor float needs drilling tonight, empty out petrol in it, seal it again. Petrol consumption is awful, and petrol dribbles down on to the engine. Oil down to one pint only.
   We stayed last night with those unpleasant people at Unilever, £2 each a night. We fought over policy, really relieving irritation at each other. Vera cried. Ursula tried at 5 o'clock this morning to

*seduce Arthur, using heavy petting and provocative positions while
he was supposed to be asleep, but wasn't. He was expected to wake,
I deduce, and, aroused, ravage her, but he declined the invitation....*

The Unilever Director, laughing, hit us for the bill. We had
$60 of CAR money which he would not accept, grinning at
our plight in trying to raise his bill in other currencies. I bet
it did not show up in Unilever's books. Nice man. We decided
to give Unilever a miss from then on.

For a while in the morning Alexa tolerated the track. It
was the usual hard stuff, dry season in the Congo, cut and
broken by old water crossings. At lunchtime I hit a bank of
sand, just after passing an army post with the crashed wreck
of an American transport plane lying on the grass under the
shadow of a Congolese flag. At first, I thought I must have
made a navigational mistake. According to our map, that post
should not have been there, and on seeing it I whipped
around and shot back the way I had come. The others were
surprised to see me racing towards them. We talked, decided
there was only one route which took us past the army base,
and then I turned around and drove through as fast as I
could. I caused a few heart failures by running out of petrol
half a mile past the post, quickly filled the tank and five
minutes later Alexa stuck in the sand.

It was a surprise, like ruefully greeting an old enemy. Sand
on route, after the desert, had not stopped me until then.
This time, of course, I had help, and with the others pushing
it was not too bad for a while. Then came a hill, deep sandy
beds, and struggling up it, my engine stopped. No starter
motor, no starting handles, wheels dug in, that was a
problem. Derek managed to manoeuvre his huge Landrover
past me eventually, and said he would tow me. But each time
the car has been towed, the bolts on the radiator have pulled
loose. When I said this, Arthur and Derek thought it must
have been a coincidence. Anyway, Alexa was towed out, the
engine started, I unhooked the rope, struggled up the rest of
the hill and waited for the others to fight their way through.

Just over the top, going downhill, cruising in third gear, I saw a rare lorry coming up. The track was narrow and the lorry, bigger than Alexa, refused to move over. Despite slipping down to first gear and turning off the engine, I found to my increasing horror that I was still rolling towards the lorry. In desperation, I headed off towards a clump of reeds, and crashed the car into it, stopping abruptly, sighing in relief and indulging in a few well chosen but I am sure unheard words at the lorry. Two miles later, having found my way back on to the road again, smoke poured out of Alexa's engine. When I looked I found no water in the radiator. The bolt on the right hand side had broken off.

I was taking the radiator out when the others drove up, thinking the cause was the towing. Later I realised it was avoiding the lorry that had done it. Arthur and Werner stayed with me. Derek and Mike drove on to the mission at Aketi. We looked at the damage. It seemed bad. After some discussion, mulling over the merits of glue or solder, we decided on the latter. My Primus stove was a heat source, and we used a screwdriver as a soldering iron. Werner did the job, much more skilfully than I could. I removed the trailing front brake cables from the car, as the connections had been smashed by rocks. Now I was truly without even the illusion of brakes. The job was finished by 5 o'clock. We had an hour to make it to the mission at Aketi, 40 kms away, before it got dark.

The sun set before we reached Aketi, but there was a full moon. Werner drove behind me, headlights full on, while Arthur played the spotlight on any ground he could see in front of me. The *piste* (I am told) became terrible. I could not see too well, but I knew it was bumpy, and natives lined along the road to look at us, attracted by the noise we made.

I found it gave me great relief to howl at the moon.

Soon, we would see the natives for a few seconds in the headlights, and then they would run away. I laughed a lot. First there was the noise of Alexa, three pistons only, sounding like a crippled coffee-grinder. She would putter by, a shadow only, silhouetted by the spotlights of the large

Swiss car behind. Then there would be this mournful howling, yip-yipping away sadly into the night. Finally, the heavy pobbling of the Citroen's exhaust pipe, minus a silencer. It was enough to give anyone a scare, never mind a Congolese who believed in tokoloshes. In this manner, we reached Aketi.

The mission did not want to know us. Derek and Mike had arrived and then gone on to Buta. That was out of the question for us. A Belgian stopped by us, as Arthur and Werner were waiting to catch Alexa while I drove in circles to slow her down, and our luck showed itself again. The Belgian's father-in-law, M. Pol Lismeau, happened to be the director for railways in the Northern Congo, and virtually owned Aketi. We were given a maison-de-passage, fed with beer and food, taken to a party, and this morning, our cars were filled with free petrol. Unbelievable. Arthur was again offered a job, his within two days if he wanted it, a contract ready in five minutes. It was difficult for him to refuse. He wanted to come back though, after he returned to Switzerland and married his girl there. The Belgians were starved of conversation, and talked half the morning, putting Miles Davis, Sidney Bechet and the Modern Jazz Quartet on the gramophone. We had a huge lunch, and reluctantly, we set off for Buta. Derek always missed the dinners. He was in so much of a hurry, poor fellow.

All the afternoon, Alexa ran well. We had been averaging one problem a day, and had come to expect a delay. But we left Aketi in the afternoon, because of the fantastic lunch, and we were anxious to make Buta by nightfall. Then Dulia appeared, and I was back on the route I had originally planned to take through the Congo. Forty-six miles to Buta. No bother with the roads. But I became aware for the first time of passing through a district which had recently seen violence. A church on our left was burnt out, the walls standing, with a jagged crack down the front. There was a way people had of looking at us, full of resentment and potential violence. There were violent signs to stop by civilians, hurriedly ignored.

As it was getting dark, the Swiss blew their horn at me. They had been flagged down by Derek, who had galloped out from his meal at the Protestant mission and just managed to catch them. Mike was there, and Vera, irritable as she is these days, Ursula with her Farmer Giles hat, and Bebronne the monkey. A young Canadian called Ray, and his American wife, were re-building the spiritual church in Buta after the terrible excesses of the Simbas. This was the town where all the missionaries were brought to be butchered and put in sacks and floated down the river. The AA routing, a million years out of date, said it had all facilities, but that was in the past tense. Death was the only present tense.

We were told stories after the others had eaten, the Swiss and I being too fat and full from our meal at Aketi to take more than a cup of tea. First, Snafu Safari has, by some incredible means, managed to get ahead of us. We had heard in Bangui that they were in Fort Lamy when we crossed the Ubangui River. Now we learned they had crossed the river at Bangassou and taken a week to cover the 251 miles here. But they were ahead of us, even if just by a day. This was galling. The missionary said they were starving, and told stories of half a banana for breakfast and a handful of rice for the rest of the day, plus tea. We belched, somewhat mollified, but we had to catch them.

I asked about the troubles in the Congo, infamous for the rape of the nuns and the cynical journalistic phrase "anyone here been raped and speaks English?" Ray told us about the fifteenth father, who lived nearby. He was a Catholic, and had been rounded up with other missionaries and brought to Buta. He was fifteenth in a queue that the Simbas were butchering with machetes. When the thirteenth father was about to be murdered, someone discovered he was a mechanic. They needed a mechanic, so they left him alive, ordering him to work immediately on a piece of equipment they had. The other fathers, including the fifteenth, were herded into a prison to await butchering the following day. The Simbas forgot to kill them, so he lived. Dying was that casual.

Arthur and Werner and I slept in an old house next to the mission. The wife of another missionary, on a visit, was plainly terrified we might be mercenaries. She needed constant reassurance from Ray. What could we say? My old car helped, but there was little else to distinguish us, other than that we did not have guns. We shaved and washed ourselves, in the hope that perhaps she would feel better seeing us do that. I thought she would be relieved to see us go.

February 3, Buta to Titule, 83 miles

Before the trip started I had pored over information the Automobile Association gave me on the Congo. I could wheel off the names of towns I would pass through – Bangassou, Bondo, Buta, Titule, Paulis, Mungbere, Mambasa, Beni – and then out into the blessed freedom of Uganda. Today was comforting for me, heading towards Titule and at last where I should be and within sight of where I knew I would be safe. There were, though, events today I would rather not live through again, if I could help it.

Derek and the others had stayed at the Catholic mission on the other side of Buta. They said they would wait there for the Swiss and me. In the morning we passed down the main street, past buildings with their windows boarded, grass growing everywhere, colours a streaky grey and dull brown, to a roundabout where we turned left for Titule. Within two minutes we were waved down by soldiers. They wanted to see our passports. We showed them, but it was not enough. We had to wait for the chief to see us. I believe he was the only one able to read. The delay made us furious; at the same time, we could look around ourselves slowly.

Buta was shocking. Wrecks of petrol stations, the shells pathetically like those we have at home. It takes a second glance to see how bad they are. I walked over to one pump. The meter showed 595482 litres, the 2 just turning so the bottom of the number 3 coming down could be seen. Who was filling his car then? What had happened? Could a petrol attendant, looking idly at the litres ticking off, have imagined the number 595482, and known that the pump would stop, forever, then?

And behind the pumps, three windows, one with a bullet hole in it, squalor and dirt. Idle irresponsible soldiers putting up their farcical display of discipline for us, all looking like they remembered a long time ago how to stand to attention, blackboards with the day's duties all marked off, everyone looking uncomfortable. Werner nursed a headache and moaned continuously. Soldiers gave us periodic orders which I countered with demands ("where's the chief?") and ignored. Arthur read the same page of *Highways of Africa* (sic) for half an hour with desperate concentration. Finally the chief arrived, glanced at our passports, and we left, heaving my car down the road to start it. We met Derek and Mike, an hour late.

I was waved on while the Swiss stopped to talk. For an hour and a half I was alone, no longer suffering the roads, just accepting them. Falling down hills, jerking over rough crude logs which pass for bridges, staggering up rain-rutted hills to another slope, time and again. At the top of one hill I became worried at smoke pouring into the cabin, and stopped. Somewhere, the radiator had busted again. The smoke was caused by the oil that usually covers the engine head, burning off the overheated engine. I waited for the others, immersed in Hemingway's *To Have and Have Not*.

Half an hour passed.

The others did not arrive. I looked up once and, along the road that is bordered on both sides by leaning jungle, I saw six black men approaching, each carrying a machete.

All the stories of this district crowded in on me. What was I to do? My attitude would be most important, for there is a smell to fear, and I had 30 seconds to compose myself and adjust my face before they reached the car. When they arrived I stepped out and was casually leaning on the open door, smoking a cigarette, my face, as far as I could manage, merely curious. They walked past slowly, staring at the car, then stopped. I said hello. One came across to me, I held out

my hand, he grabbed it and stammered....thanks. Then he
shook my thumb too, which I took to mean as a special
greeting. The others followed suit. I felt better.

What was wrong?

I said I was out of water, the radiator probably broken, and
I was waiting for my friends to come. One of them said there
was water nearby, and he ran off with my bucket to fetch
some, leaving his companions and me to stare curiously and
smile at one another. After five minutes the man returned
with a full bucket, we filled the radiator and discovered a leak
in the right bolt that Werner had soldered. That was that. It
would have to be fixed again.

With the help of the six men, each of whose black hands
followed my grubby white hand to remove the radiator, I
took it out and leaned it against a tree. Then I gave each of
them a cigarette and the man who fetched the water three
cigarettes, lit them all, and continued reading. They sat and
watched respectively. I had seen that a native who is able to
read advertises the fact by always carrying a book under his
arm. I had gone one better and was looking at the book,
turning the pages even. That, I felt, was going some, glad to
feel safe for the time being.

Finally, the others arrived. I explained the situation. Derek
had been restless ever since he had heard that Snafu Safari
were ahead of us, and he said he and Mike would go on
together, leaving the Swiss with me. We said goodbye, and
Arthur and I looked at the radiator. Werner sat in the car
with his blinding headache – the Congo has not been good to
his health.

There was very little solder left. The Swiss need it for
emergencies. We talked gloomily, before deciding to use the
same glue we had used on the timing case. The natives
watched with great interest while Arthur glued the bolt back
on, and we smoked another cigarette waiting for it to dry.
Then the radiator was put back in, bolted and sealed, we put
in water, and it worked, no leaks.

I drove off ahead while the other two cleared up after a cup
of tea. At Kimu, a soldier waved me down, not to examine

my papers, but to give me a letter he wanted to have posted in Titule, the next town. When I reached there, no one would accept the letter. I poured more petrol into the tank, looked at the sun, decided I could not make Zobia, the next town, before dark, and asked for the Catholic mission.

I was waiting by a wobbly bridge when the Swiss arrived.

A lorry was backed to the bridge, and natives were carrying sacks across it to another lorry headed towards Bambesa. Arthur and I walked across the bridge, watching pieces fall off it into the river. We reached the mission, which was half a mile further on. We were given a room each, and walked back to find the bridge cleared. The drive across it was interesting, full of creaks and shakes. That bridge will not last much longer. So long as it lasts until tomorrow morning, I do not mind.

This mission is the most peaceful I have been at, with one white father and a black brother, and the country falling away from the terrace to the jungle. Werner has gone straight to bed without eating. I have had a beer, and will eat now. How quiet it is.

February 4/5, Titule to Isiro (Paulis), 215 miles

Still on the road, plagued by punctures, with just over 600 miles to go to Kampala, and perhaps 400 to Uganda. My luck has been roaring away at full power, despite small setbacks. We are at the beginning of the last stage to Uganda.

Yesterday morning, both remaining members of the Grauenhaft Safari, Arthur's Citroen and my poor battered Austin 7, left the Catholic mission at Titule. The father there, a calm man, at peace with his surroundings now, saw us off. It was a different matter three years ago when he fled the dreaded Simbas. I have found out exactly what Simbas are, at last. They are tribesmen here in the North East Congo who drink together and take drugs and then go out to loot and pillage. They are quiet now, and said to be resting.

The father wished us Godspeed, and walked away to his primary school where 3,500 children are being taught; there are also 200 children at secondary school here. We picked our way over the wobbly bridge, boards creaking, small pieces still falling into a wide sluggish river, and set off for Poko.

We had been told that the roads were bad. They were, but not too bad. Without brakes, I whined downhill in second gear, the car yawing like a broken-backed old boat. Sometimes I could see the red and white Citroen in the mirror. Most times I drove alone. Going up the hill that usually follows a down is nerve-racking. I never know whether I will have enough power. It usually happens that I crawl the last few yards in shrieking first gear. Smoke pours into the cabin, ignored now unless it becomes really thick. It has been doing that on and off since France.

At noon I had a puncture. I could not find the second tyre lever in my tool bag, and anyway the jack has never fitted under the back axle without someone lifting the car, so I waited for the Swiss. Werner was lying sick in the front seat when they arrived. He was pretty sarcastic. Why did I prefer talking to white people (the father at Mission Titule) at nights instead of mending my spare tyre? I was sarcastic back, but he was right, and I eventually apologised. My slow speed is getting on all our nerves.

I mended the puncture alone, sweating about two pints of water, and crawled on.

That night, last night, after a long steep hill, we slept at a Catholic mission, run by Germans. They gave us two bottles of beer, and put us into a partially completed building. Our morale was very bad. I found that the inner tube on my spare tyre has had the valve torn off. I will try, without much hope, to mend it. It leaves me with four wheels only, and some 400 miles of rotten track to go. We ate a soup, my only meal for the day, and made some tea. Arthur said he could smell my clutch from his car, 200 yards behind me. He said for the first time that he did not think I could make Kampala. He suggested I leave the car in Poko and go with them to get a new clutch and engine parts, and then come back and fit them. I said no.

Breakfast was a cup of tea and a piece of dried bread. I changed a faulty valve on the rear right tyre while eating, and at 8 o'clock, we set off towards Paulis. A bridge we had been warned about was not as dangerous as the bridge at Titule, but the drop was deeper and the river was fast-flowing. I drove like the clappers all morning, sometimes reaching 30 mph, until 1 o'clock, when the right rear tyre punctured again. This happened three times in 10 miles. The last time Arthur drove away with the inner tube and had it repaired at a nearby mission.

I finished *To Have and Have Not*, sweat pouring off me, shuffling to catch some shade under one tree. An African sat by me for a while, then gave me a huge bunch of bananas, "as a present" he said, when I protested. He pushed the car when the tyre was re-fitted, I gave him a cigarette and he seemed happy.

Two men came up to me in Paulis while I was looking for the petrol station. They were white, Monsieur Moro and Monsieur Le Maire; they looked like mercenaries, extremely tough. They told us Derek and Mike and Snafu Safari had left town this afternoon, just before we arrived. They have taken the northern route. M. Moro said it would be best to put our cars on a train from here to Mungbere, then head south to Beni. The other route added 600 kms, plus a chance of meeting Sudanese tribesmen out on a wing-ding. We are staying tonight in a lovely house with a hot bath. I have been offered a job (as had Arthur and Werner, of course) as a crop-spraying pilot for three months in a year. I would have to get my licence in order again. I wondered how Fiona would go for that, a 3-month contract in the Congo at the end of the year? The money, £400 a month, was excellent. But they are probably shooting the bull anyway, and the offer was likely not to be a real one.

If we could get the train, we would probably reach Kampala before all the others. In the morning we would see. Kampala seemed very near. I knew that the clutch could go, or the transmission buckle, at any time, ending it all. But there was not far to go. I just needed a little more luck.

February 6, static, 37,531 miles on the clock, maison de passage, Paulis (Isiro)

We arrived in Paulis yesterday. Tomorrow morning we are leaving for Mungbere. The rumours in this fearful town have driven us from pillar to post. Arthur is impatient for action and will believe nothing. I am apprehensive. We are told that the route to Mungbere is impassable for trucks, and absolutely impassable for my little car. Today is Thursday, and if we wait until Sunday, our cars will be put on a train, free of charge because the train director likes us, and transported to Mungbere. This is said to be normal procedure for all the trucks going to Uganda. And yet, five minutes later, we are told that brewery trucks have just come up the "impassable" road. It is confusing.

This morning we spent gathering information, wondering whether to drive on or take the train. There were two choices of road. One goes east to Mungbere, south to Mambasa, Kommanda, Beni and out, 387 miles to the border, 672 miles to Kampala. The other goes north and east through Dungu, Faradjem Aba, Arua, and out, 358 miles to the border, 832 to Kampala. Naturally we favoured the first route, but the Belgians here took great pleasure in reciting all the reasons why it is impossible to drive. Snafu Safari, Derek and Mike have apparently taken the northern route. If we can get through to Mungbere, it is possible we may beat them to Kampala, a prospect which tickles me.

I met two girls at the director's house, both English. They were with Snafu Safari, but had opted to stay behind and make their own way south. The girl I talked to told me a pack of lies. Oh yes, she said, Siafu will be in Nairobi by now. No, it had been an absolutely lovely trip, and she professed not to understand why I thought there had been any trouble, or that Tim, the leader, had made his arrangements as he went along. Yes, they were going to stay in Paulis for a while and then take an aeroplane to Nairobi.

I wondered if the journey had affected her wits. There were no aeroplanes flying between Paulis and Nairobi. I found one roundabout aerial route which would cost the same as an air-ticket from London to Kenya, but she had no money, so how would she pay to take it? And I knew where Snafu was, almost to the mile. When she was speaking to me they were 130 miles north of us, heading east. As for Tim's arrangements, how relieved I am that I did not take that British consul's advice in Algiers and attempt to stick with them. Tim's one saving point, and it is a big one, is that his group is still on the road, despite all its troubles. For the two girls, it would only take a little time for them to see how difficult their situation was. Perhaps another safari would pass through, and they could join that. Poor innocents.

Alexa has been primed ready to go since this morning, but I was reluctant to leave. The Swiss were impatient. We were tied together, creditor and debtor, and with some fatalism I would drive on. We spent the evening listening to bongo drums, hollow and babbling, like a stream over rocks, while the Belgians told us blood-curdling stories...."there was this Simba came at us, high as a kite, drugged and drunk, with a machete. The mercenary with us had a machine-gun, and fired a burst, hitting the Simba about the chest. But the Simba took it, just took it, and carried on towards us. The mercenary sprayed the Simba with bullets" – realistic mime of the grimace on the Simba's face as the bullets hit him – "but he kept on coming. The mercenary was afraid, and I was too. In the end the Simba had to be shot to pieces before he would stop" – hand shaking loosely from the wrist to signify amazement, and we all took another drink of our beers.

Out in the backyard Alexa is in need only of this typewriter and my sleeping bag to be ready. Her front mudguards are tied together across the bonnet with a piece of rope, and the rope is kept from slipping by another drawn over the roof and tied to the rear bumper. I have a little oil left, and must make an effort to find some more. She is sure to use all I have before we reach Uganda. I wished, uselessly, that we could wait for the train. Such a little way to go, after so long. There is nothing else to do but play my luck and watch it run. Should it last the next few days, I am out into

the clear, to money, to independence, and perhaps again to
that purity of feeling I had in the desert when there was just
me and the car and the sand. With 7,300 miles behind us,
what is another 400?

February 7, Paulis to Mungbere, 88 miles

Arthur and Werner and one of the Belgians pushed Alexa
down the small slope at the back of the maison-de-passage,
I threw in second gear, and she started. We drove out of
town, losing our way once, then finding the road to
Mungbere. The usual amount of smoke poured into the
cabin, but as the day went on it did not stop.

The road was not as bad as we had expected. Lies again.
We heard them all the time in the Congo. It should have been
possible to make Mungbere by early afternoon and then on
to the mission at Andudu to sleep there. Two hours passed.
I kept leaning out of the window to avoid the fumes. At
around 11 o'clock, M. Moro would be flying back from
Mungbere, looking for us. If we were in trouble, we were to
leave a white patch on the roof of my car.

At 10.30am the engine lost power. Two pistons only were
working. I stopped and looked at the engine. Oil, fresh oil,
was sprayed over the crank-case and starting motor. Arthur
came up for a look, and we push-started the car, listening to
the engine. It sounded sicker than ever. I removed the oil-
filler cap and listened. There was a sonk-sonk-sonk noise,
the same as in Fort Lamy, 2000 miles back.

"The rings on number 4 piston have gone," said Arthur.
"Oil is coming up into the firing chamber and stopping the
plug from firing."

We took off the plug. It was covered in oil. Arthur took off
the other two plugs and cleaned them, and put them back
into the engine. Just then, M. Moro came over, passing in
circles for five minutes while we waved and took useless
photographs. I was feeling more and more detached. We left
no white patch on Alexa's roof, and the aircraft flew away.

"What are you going to do?" asked Arthur.

"Burn her. Let's look for a place."

We drove on. Suddenly, three pistons started working again, and I began to hope. Is it too much to stop every 20 miles and clean the plugs, until we reach Uganda? No, I thought. But there was another noise that was even more ominous. I stopped the car and we all listened.

"Rev the engine," said Arthur. I revved the engine. "Hmmmm, a big end is going."

The car's clutch had been weak for 500 miles. Working on two pistons, sometimes three, a big-end going, no brakes, the front spring with three leaves smashed again, little oil left, no lights....

"You don't mind if she takes a long time to die?" I asked.

"No."

We drove on, 20 miles, 25 miles, back to two pistons again. Suddenly the clouds opened up and it lashed with rain. It poured for 20 minutes. There was not enough power for me to drive. Werner put his Citroen behind and pushed Alexa up a slight slope, and I rolled down the other side. Three pistons started working again, but I was now facing the situation. I could not drive through to Kampala. Yet that scoffing in Paulis, that Alexa would never make Mungbere, rankled. We drove on, passing places where it would have been possible to burn the car without setting alight to the countryside. I had a carnet de passage, and I thought to get an official in Mungbere to witness the destruction of the car, so I would not forfeit the import duty of £200 which an insurance company in London was liable for. An official could stamp the carnet, legally clearing me. The speedometer clock passed 37,600 mile mark, and at 4 o'clock we struggled into Mungbere.

I asked for the mission. When we got there, keeping the engine running, I sat in Alexa and inquired about the father. He was away. We said we would wait. I was feeling miserable. Driving into town, the engine whining in third gear, missing and firing, she sounded like she was sobbing. The noise affected me so that I had consciously to think of something else. An African came up and said there was a

Swiss planter in town. I let the engine stop. As it happened, though I did not know it then, it would never run again.

We were conducted to the planter's house in the Citroen. Arthur drove, with the African next to him and me next to the African, Werner sitting in the back. I left Alexa inside the compound of the mission. The planter, M. Von Wild, was expecting us. Moro had told him we were coming through. Von Wild gave us a beer while we told him about our situation. He looked dubious about the carnet.

"An African would not understand," he said.

He tried out an explanation on an African teacher who was drinking with us. I followed the whole thing and thought it was expressed very clearly, but the African doubted that I would be given permission to burn the car. Never mind, I said, an official would be sure to understand. We went to see the local chief. He listened, seemed reasonably intelligent, nodded agreeably when I said I was going to burn her, and said he wanted to look at the car. We drove to the mission. He whistled at Alexa's age and appearance, and asked if she could run again. I lied, and said she could not. Perhaps she would run for another 10 miles, but what business was it of his? Nevertheless, he suggested quite calmly that I should drive the 80 miles back to Paulis and see the customs post there. I rejected his advice. Would he sign the carnet witnessing destruction? He would, he said, though he wished to point out that he was only a minor official. Anyone with a stamp would do. I wanted it over quickly. Von Wild towed Alexa to the airfield. He ran over a rut and the rope snapped.

"This place is as good as any," he said.

I thought so too, and began to take out what I wanted. Then the official spoke again. He would not allow me to burn my car. There might be trouble. No, he would not have it destroyed. Nothing must be burned in the Congo. I was to leave it just as it was after removing what I wanted. I became very angry, so that Arthur had to physically restrain me, and Werner flapped around worrying that I would hit the official.

"If you burn the car," said Von Wild, "you will be put in

prison. I will be too, for aiding you. This is Africa, you know, not Europe."

I agreed bitterly, and turned to the Congolese official, who was hanging on to the shreds of his dignity. Stupid man, fearful as we found all officials are fearful of putting their names to anything, afraid of a comeback. I looked at him and told him in English that I thought he was a cheat, two-faced, a liar, and I was hauled off before I could finish. Von Wild hurriedly drove the official away. I did not see him again.

There were Africans around Alexa. It made me furious to see that. They were waiting to see what I would leave, and then they would fall on her themselves and tear her to pieces. Captain Bebronne's threat came back to me. Bloody Congo, it got her finally. I drove the Africans off and threatened them and went back to sit in the car.

It was getting dark. Arthur said gently that I should get my things out. I began to remove small parts, the patent plaque on the dashboard, the speedometer, starting handle, wiper motor, battery, things I had lived with for so long. Arthur helped me quietly. He knew how I was feeling. It was his own Citroen that we had burned between Chad and the CAR.

Finally, everything I wanted was out, some to be given to Von Wild for his help, and to exchange for cigarettes, some to be sold to Greek traders in the area, some to continue with me to South Africa. I took a few photos by the lights and spotlight of the Citroen, but it was probably too dark for them to turn out. In the background, always, the Africans hovered, waiting for me to leave.

So now I must finish my beer, and stop my conversation – a poor thing anyway at this moment – with Von Wild's mother. She was the widow of a Luftwaffe general in the last war, living in a house with faded bloodstains where a Belgian and his wife were murdered by Simbas in the troubles earlier in the decade. I was in a state of surface intoxication, and inner stillness. We talked about the (second world) war, while in the back of my mind I thought, Alexa is truly finished. There is room for me in the Citroen through to

Kampala. From there I will fly on to Johannesburg, if an aircraft service runs between black and white Africa. I have no feelings at all at the moment, aside from a false and temporary feeling of relief at the lifting of responsibility for the car. But 300 miles, that is all it is to Uganda and safety. We have to drive out of Von Wild's house and down the road past the airfield where Alexa is lying. I do not want to see her. We should all move now. Say goodbye and go. It is funny not feeling anything at all.

 **Afterword**

We decided to get out of the Congo as quickly as possible. Arthur drove first, through the night, until 2 o'clock, when Werner took over. I sat in the third seat behind the driver and watched the lightning over mountains to the east.

Once we stopped.

"Too heavy," said Arthur.

He walked around the car and poked at the equipment on the roof-rack. I said my tent could go; we threw it by the side of the road, along with one spare tyre. We drove on, half asleep, until the dawn.

It was foggy when we passed through Mambasa, east towards Kommanda, along a fair track. Then the sun came up and the jungle steamed for an hour, so that we had to keep stopping to clear the windscreen.

It felt peculiar to stop at will.

At 8 o'clock we turned south again, towards Beni, thinking we would be there in three hours, and perhaps in Kampala that night. The rains were starting though, and soon we hit mud. Someone – was it me? – said "Alexa would not have got through here". The first large trough held us up for an hour and a half. On the left, the road dipped through ankle-deep mud to a depth of 7 feet, while on the right some slippery logs provided a kind of bridge. One of the Citroen's wheels caught between the logs, there was a crunching sound and we were stuck. Eventually, a large truck pulled us out backwards, by brute force. We tried again, down the muddy dip, stuck there too, heaved the car out, backwards again. In the end we re-built the log bridge entirely, putting in props to hold the logs together, and then Arthur drew back and, alone, flew at the bridge. He nearly did not make it, but when he got through Werner and I threw ourselves into the still-moving car. A hundred yards later there was another nearly impossible stretch of mud. We learned in Kampala that Derek and Mike came along this same route and gave up, turning back to go by Murchison Falls.

In 8 hours, from 8 o'clock in the morning until 4 o'clock in the afternoon, we covered 20 miles. There was one stretch where the mud and ruts continued for 300 yards. Arthur always drove them alone, because of his great skill at the wheel. Werner and I walked. It was hot, but the flies were not as bad as at other times. In that long stretch, Arthur shot from the left side of the road to the right, back to the left, skidding and yawing, and plumped both left wheels of the car into a rain-filled ditch two and a half feet deep. A convoy of trucks drove by – unlike those in the desert they did not stop to help, just palmed their biceps at us and roared on. We were becoming tired, driven up-tight with each other. Each of us had a solution to the problem, but the angle of the car was such that the engine was starved of petrol. It soon stopped.

"It's impossible now," said Werner.

I ground my teeth in rage.

"Nothing is impossible," I snarled. Not the best of times for all of us.

We tied a long rope, wound around a pulley, between the welded roof-rack of the car and a nearby tree, and hauled the car more upright. This brought petrol back to the engine, which fired again. Then, like the weight at the end of a pendulum, and with the help of some Africans, Arthur drove furiously to lift the car out of the ditch.

It was OK after that, and our tempers cooled.

At Beni we found a hotel. The people there were pathetically pleased to see us, though the Citroen looked a mess and we were all covered in flaking dried mud. Beni is the nearest Congolese town to the Albert National Park, which competes with Elizabeth Park in Uganda for tourists. Beni does not do very well, but it tries hard with the few tourists it gets. After 40 hours awake, broken by cat-naps, it was easy to sleep that night. We were late up next morning.

There were clouds around the Ruwenzori Mountains when we drove through the park to Kasindi and the border. It looked like it might rain. The customs post was a little bothersome, and one man wanted my typewriter, but we were offhand and confident so near to Uganda, and passed through within half an hour. Later, by Lake Edward, we had a beer and looked at dozens of hippos rising for their evening wallow. I had a splitting headache.

Aside from those rotten sardines in the desert, it was the first time I had been ill on the journey.

We drove through the darkness, past lightning again, huge jagged columns marching from north to south, in sequence. At 10 o'clock we reached Mbarara, and tarmac again. I had abandoned Alexa just 50 hours earlier.

From Mbarara to Kampala, I drove the Citroen. Entering the city, a special police patrol stopped us. It was lovely to talk to them in English. Afterwards, we drove along Kampala Road to a place near the university, hauled out our sleeping bags, and fell asleep on a dirt patch opposite a petrol station. We had arrived.

I saw the bank later in the morning, drawing out the money which had been sent to me, and paying the Swiss the £70 they had grub-staked me. Austin's commiserated with me over the car, and gave me £1 for two photos. One newspaper took an article. I needed money for my air fare. For two nights I camped with the Swiss. Derek and Mike found us, and the remnants of the Grauenhaft Safari talked over all that had happened.

Without a car, I did not belong anymore, and was

impatient to leave. There was a flight, London – Entebbe (21 miles south of Kampala) – Johannesburg, on Wednesday, February 12. That was one day before the guess-arrival date I had sent to Fiona from Kano, Nigeria. I took the flight after telegraphing Fiona. I also sent a telegram to the *Irish Independent*, telling them I did not make it, and articles would follow. Fiona was waiting for me at Johannesburg, nervous after a 4-hour delay. We were almost strangers, shy with two different lives apart for nearly 20 months....

 **Loose Ends**

What Happened to them all?

There are a few loose ends. People came into my life, stayed there a short while, and then disappeared. Through the months and years following the journey, people I had met in those peculiar circumstances contacted me in South Africa, and back in England. This is what I learned:

Arthur Lang and Werner Streiff - the two surviving Swiss went on with Derek to Nairobi, appeared on television there, had a holiday, then sold their car and all their equipment and flew back to Switzerland. Their girlfriends were waiting there to marry them. Marilyn never did send the £50 she owed them.

Derek and Vera Haldane - continued on down to South Africa, where I met them. We visited a few times, and once had a party at a house they had rented. They planned to take a boat over to South America, shipping their beautifully-equipped Landrover, and drive up to the USA.

Meinhard "Mike" Wagenschein - the huge German teacher had his Citroen 2CV broken into in the camping site in Kampala two days after I left, and was robbed of everything, including his passport and travellers cheques. I last heard he was lobbying the efficient German consul to get help.

Ursula Carmen - came down to South Africa with Derek. I met her at a party, with her usual man in tow, and she was all beams and smiles. She returned to England after six months.

Siafu (Snafu) Safari - eventually made it to Johannesburg, where it hurriedly disbanded. Tim Bailey, the leader, ran up numerous debts, and proposed to meet them by organising another safari and driving back to London.

Robert Auberson - the Swiss with the modified Citroen I had met in Spain, went across the desert track to Tamanrasset with Siafu, and then continued with Derek, but was turned back at the border with Niger because he had no visa. Last heard of driving furiously to Niamey to pick up a visa.

The Scruffs - Bob, Stuart and Mick – apparently the British consul in Algiers flew down to Tamanrasset and saved them driving their wrecked van up the Hoggar Trail. I received a message just before I left Nigeria that Bob and Stuart were going to hitch "after me", and they would meet me in South Africa. I never saw them. According to the message, Mick went straight home.

Tom and Dorothy Pearson and family – I had left them in the camping site at Algeciras near Gibraltar, camped out in their 3-tonner. Thirty years later, having become the first person to fly a microlight aircraft around the world in 1998, I had a letter from Dorothy, now living in France, written two days after I had finished the flight. She wrote to me at the Reform Club, where I had become a member: "My 3 sons accompanied you into the town to help you obtain rope, bucket and sundries before you actually took off. We thought you were the most charismatic person we had ever met. Over the years we have heard of your other escapades and achievements, and applauded you all the way…it's really marvellous to know that you have not changed in your adventurous attitude to life even though the years have passed. I still see that young enthusiastic chap who sat on the ground in a camp-site in Spain all those years ago, poring over maps of the Sahara Desert and talking about everything under the sun!"

The Cowboys - Paul, Brian and Ian – I had left them in Maiduguri, Nigeria, where Paul had malaria. When he recovered he was too apprehensive of the Congo to continue, and returned to Europe. Brian and Ian hitched (!) through the Congo and joined Derek Haldane for a short while in Nairobi. They made their own way south to South Africa, Ian with his precious bag of tools, Brian full of confidence and "making it with tons of chicks". They met me in Johannesburg six months after I arrived, and were planning to go to Japan for Expo 70.

Jackie - Welsh girl repatriated from Kano who carried my letters home. She met my parents, went around to see my friends, impressing everyone with her enormous personality. Thought to have returned to her civil service job to pay back her air fare to the British Government, and then – no doubt at all – she would be off again somewhere.

Roger Phelps and Freddie Hammerle - Englishman in Thames van who left Kano with Swiss friend of Arthur and Werner. They reached Bangui two weeks before us, but were unable to persuade the ferryman to take them across the Ubangui River. Left Bangui three days before we arrived, drove to Yaounde, sold the van and bought two air tickets to Johannesburg. For weeks after their arrival they were unable to find jobs, so they hitch-hiked to Cape Town. Roger was broke, and returned to England by boat. Freddie intended to return to Zurich, but found a job as a barman in Cape Town, and stayed. He wrote to me after some articles on Alexa appeared in the Johannesburg *Sunday Times.*

Ray Saunders - the American we had left in Fort Lamy, did not return to Europe, but was reported seen in Nairobi by Siafu Safari. He cut them dead. It was rumoured that he intended to sue Tim Bailey, Siafu's leader, for alleged false advertising and numerous other alleged offences.

Captain Gaston Bebronne - Years later, in London, when I worked for the BBC as a radio reporter, I came across a journalist who was an expert on those troubled years in the former Belgian Congo, and asked about Bebronne. He was, I heard, a tremendous killer of men, responsible for dozens of deaths in the heat and rage of battle. But he was also an idealist, with his yearning to be a modern-day Lawrence of Arabia. I never discovered if he went back to Belgium and resumed an army career in peace-time Europe. It would have bored him.

Me and Fiona - I was visited four days after I arrived in South Africa by the Security Police. They spent forty-five minutes drinking tea to ask me if I was a liberal. I said that, like any Englishman, *of course* I was a liberal (who wasn't?). Ten days later they returned and spent another forty-five minutes drinking tea, to ask me if I was a communist. I said I wasn't; how could I be a communist if I was a liberal? I worked first as a (not very good at the time) reporter on the Johannesburg *Sunday Times*, then as a science feature writer for the *Rand Daily Mail*, and also as a Johannesburg correspondent for the *Irish Independent*. I believe the authorities took exception to one article I wrote, because on August 27, 1969, while Fiona and I were writing our wedding invitations, the Security Police again turned up on our doorstep and ordered me out of the country. They used to expel six priests and six journalists a year, under *Apartheid*, pour encourager les autres.

We were married the following year, in England.

I would like to say we lived happily ever afterwards, but we parted after 24 years, her shout, and were divorced five years later. We have two beautiful children, James and Jade, who are also attracted to Africa, for all its deeply corrupt faults. In the meantime, I have had a number of other adventures.